The Alchemy

of Touch

Moving Towards Mastery
Through the Lens of Zero Balancing

Fritz Frederick Smith, MD

COMPLEMENTARY
MEDICINE PRESS

Taos, New Mexico 2005

Alchemy of Touch
Moving Towards Mastery
Through the Lens of Zero Balancing

Fritz Frederick Smith, MD

© 2005 Fritz Frederick Smith
Complementary Medicine Press
Distributed by Redwing Book Company
202 Bendix Drive, Taos NM 87571
www.redwingbooks.com

Library of Congress Cataloging-in-Publication Information

Smith, Fritz Frederick, 1929-
  The alchemy of touch : moving towards mastery through the lens of zero balancing /
Fritz Frederick Smith.
    p. ; cm.
  Includes index.
  ISBN 0-9673034-6-X (trade pbk. : alk. paper)
  1. Touch--Therapeutic use. 2. Energy--Therapeutic use. 3. Vital force--Therapeutic use.
4. Mind and body.
  [DNLM: 1. Acupressure--methods. 2. Complementary Therapies. 3. Mind-Body Rela-
tions (Metaphysics) WB 369.5.A17 S647a 2005] I. Title.
  RZ999.S65 2005
  615.8'22--dc22

                                                    2005033594

Cover image: "Mountain Fire," pastel, © 2002 Fritz Frederick Smith

Library of Congress Number: 2005033594
International Standard Book Number (ISBN): ISBN 0-9673034-6-X

Printed in the United States of America

Alchemy of Touch is not intended as a Zero Balancing instruction manual. Many
ideas presented here are taken from Zero Balancing to illustrate general principles
found in energy work and touch. Procedures are presented in a stand-alone fashion
to illustrate principles, but they are still powerful and should only be used with
good judgment. In actual practice they are done as part of a full Zero Balancing
session, when and where appropriate, and are not used as isolated techniques.

Dedicated to

Aminah Raheem

Acknowledgements

First and foremost I want to thank Deirdre Burton, without whom there would be no Alchemy of Touch. She has been a true friend, instrumental in making this book a reality, from our first discussions in Mexico, to her organizing and then hosting the original eight of us for a week in her home. In addition, Deirdre was a tremendous help in editing my work and helping me surmount moments of writer's block.

I am deeply grateful to those folks who gathered at Deirdre's home for seven memorable days of focused work and creativity: Deirdre herself, Tom Davis, Carl, Sara Conkey, Alan Hext, Richard Beaumont, and John Hamwee.

Many thanks to Tom Davis for his computer and writing skills, and to Hal Zina Bennett, Jim Oschman and Jackie O'Hanlon for their editorial feedback and help.

Thanks to Bill Weintraub for introducing me to my publisher.

My endless gratitude goes to Bob Felt and Martha Fielding of Redwing Book Company for their publishing skills, editorial guidance, and for holding the space for me to write the book at my own pace.

Through the whole eight-year process of the book's gestation and creation, I was, and continue to be, infinitely grateful to Aminah Raheem, my partner and wife, for her unending support, editorial reflections, and willingness just to let me be at my computer writing.

Finally, I want to give a special thanks to my many friends, teachers, patients, and workshop participants who have added to and shared in this journey with me.

Table of Contents

Foreword

First World Western technological sophistication gives us greater comfort and physical health and there is an unspoken assumption that: information is power. The more we know about something and the way it works, the more power we believe we have.

As founder and editor-in-chief of *Kindred Spirit* magazine for seventeen years, I have had more information pouring through me than most in the field of holistic concepts, complementary healthcare and contemporary spirituality. As a dedicated investigator of the cutting edge of Mind, Body and Spirit subjects I know one thing: Information is *not* power. You can be deeply informed in any of the above areas, but still you can operate at a deeply unconscious level. It takes humility, and an unerring focus on the truth to truly meet the powerful within you ... and that takes a quality of heart that allows love to be at the center of your life.

Fritz Smith, the founder of Zero Balancing and author of this book, is one of the most heart-centered, truth-centered beings I have ever had the enormous good fortune to call friend. He is also one of the most humble men I know, and has an unquestionable integrity; I have never seen him act inappropriately or from outside a space of respect for those he meets.

The eruption of Zero Balancing as a healing modality in the world came to Fritz as a direct revelation. No matter how his medically trained mind and clarity of thought may lead you think otherwise, I believe it's important to acknowledge that, at its source, Zero Balancing was received from a higher level of consciousness. Fritz has honed it into a remarkably effective tool for freeing people of the dense energy patterns that reside undetected in our bodies.

A Zero Balancing session is, almost always, a pleasurable experience and one that holds the possibility of positively altering the course of our lives.

Fritz gave me my first session following an interview for the magazine in 1991. I felt complete with the interview and my ability to convey to the readers an accurate explanation of the modality. I was ready to leave. Fritz insisted he give me a session. Despite my tendency to rush off and maintain my busy schedule I agreed. Forty minutes later my life was changed forever. Controlling energy patterns set deep within the structure of my bones (that I was completely unaware of) were removed. I felt a level of profound peace and happiness that was beyond words. And most important of all, in this brand new sense of who I was, there was Fritz. His eyes softly and lovingly looking directly at me, making sure that I was in a fit state to rejoin the world.

A year later, when there was no interview to be done, out of the blue, Fritz rings me and offers to give me another session. To drop everything I was doing at the time was inappropriate to the meeting of deadlines and the number of plates I was spinning in my business. When is it ever appropriate to dive deeply into yourself? When isn't it? With Fritz's soft invitation lingering on the phone, everything I was doing fell to its appropriate level; I agreed. That session cemented my fate. Again it was a deeply satisfying and transformative experience. I chose to stay with Fritz and his students and join them in an evening meal that night. In response to Fritz's second invitation I agreed to become a student of his and learn Zero Balancing for myself. For the next nine years Zero Balancing became a key part of my life. (I also met my life partner on that first ZB training course!) I learnt the importance and power of clear touch. My body changed radically. More freedom came into my life; indeed I became more available to myself and those around me. Zero Balancing can facilitate a flow of extraordinary non-mental content that comes from subtle energy changes, and in such moments portals of inspiration and truth are opened that can never be closed. Indeed Fritz showed himself to be a true mentor to me. His wisdom, as you will see, shines through this book. His work, which already benefits hundreds of thousands of clients worldwide, will continue to inform and transform future generations in the deep truth of clear touch.

Fritz's first book, *Inner Bridges,* has, since its publication, been a valuable textbook for all those in complementary health care and energetic medicine, as it is, in my opinion, the primary book that actually tells us how to touch energy.

Alchemy of Touch was born in a rather different way. Invitations were sent out to various Zero Balancing students and teachers and those in the media to spend seven days together. There was a fixed protocol (Fritz always has a firm structure, to act as a crucible, from which a true alchemy can blossom). In the mornings Fritz would read a first draft chapter of his proposed book. Radically new and exciting ideas were aired—it was a fantastically creative time. He would then invite discussion. Later in the day he would give a session to one of those assembled. We all witnessed these sessions and my job was to write down exactly what I saw was happening. Each fulcrum, breath, change of expression, exchange of words, and Fritz's own description of what he was doing, was recorded. The person receiving the session also wrote up their account of what happened later the same day.

This book has been a long time coming; none of us are truly in control of the timing of such things. But you can now read the final version of all that happened, and the depth of wisdom that sparked it. But I wish to share with you, that in the middle of what I know to be truly higher forces that surrounded us all in those magical days, there was a point, sitting out in the garden during a break, that I suddenly found tears flooding down my cheeks. I had become so overwhelmed by the profundity of what I had witnessed during one of those sessions that tears just had to be released. Simply as a witness I remember this book project as a time of indescribable happiness and joy. I felt the fire of aliveness against a background of deep peace and let go. It remains a keynote experience against which to assess the value of my present use of time in leading my life in a creative and loving way.

Fritz and I share a love of surprises. As you read this book there will be many surprises. You will learn about energy in your own body and see its consequences played out in your life and in the lives of those around you. You cannot work correctly with energy and not see it mirrored all around you. This is a deeply informative and radically transformative book. You, like me, will not "come off the table" of reading it and be the same person. After all, we don't hear, see or think touch, we *experience* it.

The knowledge and wisdom in this book can be a higher plateau to experience life at an elevated level, to experiment with becoming conscious of energy in a much deeper way. Remember: information isn't power — but here we are shown the doorway through which we can walk into a more fulfilled life and, for practitioners, an effective way to assist clients further in their own evolution. Fritz will touch you with his words, as surely as if he had touched you with his hands. Enjoy your new life.

Richard Beaumont
Founder and Editor-in-Chief, *Kindred Spirit Magazine*
May 2004

Introduction

Touch is perhaps the oldest and still most reliable healing modality that we possess. *Alchemy of Touch* explores principles and ways of increasing the power and effectiveness of touch by coupling it with heightened fields of energy and vibration. It is written for the person curious about the underpinnings of health and healing, and for the therapist interested in the relationship of touch to the body, to the mind, and to the spirit.

The empowerment of touch is a natural extension of the body/mind healing system of Zero Balancing (ZB), which I formulated in the early 1970s. *Alchemy of Touch* is meant to be a book bigger than Zero Balancing itself. However, since many of the ideas and possibilities presented here come from my first-hand therapeutic experience and from the Zero Balancing perspective, it is important to give a brief overview of the Zero Balancing system.

ZB is a hands-on body/mind therapy, which follows a proto-col lasting thirty to forty-five minutes, administered to a patient horizontally reclined and comfortably but fully attired. It com-bines an Eastern view of energy and healing with a Western view of medicine and science. It is based on the quantum physics perspec-tive that the particle and the wave are the two fundamental aspects that comprise our universe. In terms of the human being, I have translated this principle to signify the structure and energy of the body. Zero Balancing is a non-diagnostic system of healing. It has the stated objective to improve the balance between the structure and energy within a person's system, with the understanding that this promotes greater health and actualization.

Zero Balancing is an ideal vehicle for exploring touch and its alchemical possibilities because it is based on principles of nature rather than on medical models of symptoms and disease. One ad-vantage of a non-symptom oriented healing system is that we can focus on a person's health, potential, and actualization, and not be limited to symptom care. Working with a person's potential signifi-cantly deepens our understanding of touch.

The initial impetus for writing this book began as a dream in Mexico when a dear friend, Deirdre Burton, suggested that we gather a group of people together for a concentrated period to talk about energy and structure, do Zero Balancing sessions, and see what that mix would bring. Nine months later eight of us gathered at Deirdre's home in England and spent the next seven days explor-ing the potentials of ZB, extending our thinking into alchemical possibilities. At that time I gave each person a ZB session. We re-corded my comments, the observation of the session, and the re-ceiver's comments and reflections. These sessions are reported here in detail. In some cases I was able, eight years later, to contact the person involved and get an update from them about how the ses-sion had played out in the intervening years.

The ZB sessions I've chosen for this book may give the mis-leading impression that we talk at great length during a session and that only one session is given or needed. On the contrary, in actual practice the majority of ZB sessions are performed with minimal talk. Similarly, in actual practice, a series of sessions is more the rule than the exception; many people come in for a routine visit each month. The examples I present here were either in workshop settings, or in the creation of the book, where more talking was appropriate and only one session was possible. The outcome of doing a even single session, however, shows the potential power of touch.

What helps make touch alchemical is the ability to translate an intellectual or esoteric concept or idea into an actual experience for someone else. As you shall see in the course of reading the book, the wisdom and understanding of great teachers and healers can be viewed through the lens of ZB, and translated into a direct experience. For instance, Shinzen Young, a Buddhist Vispassna meditation teacher, says that pain multiplied by resistance leads to suffering. Applying his formula, we can release resistance of the body/mind through touch and thereby directly reduce suffering. Or, as I will later describe, we can use touch to activate a meditative experience similar to those described by teachers such as Deepak Chopra or Joseph Campbell. Or we can use touch to seek our true nature as described by Ramana Maharshi or the Dali Lama.

For this book I made the decision to use standard anatomical terms as well as some terms that are unique to Zero Balancing. To assist readers unfamiliar with these terms, I have included a glossary, which you'll find in the appendix of the book, where I have also included diagrams of the skeleton and an outline of the Zero Balancing protocol. I believe these resources will make your reading of the book more enjoyable and meaningful. I want to be clear that while I have made many references to ZB, this book is not intended to be a how-to text for doing Zero Balancing. Rather, I have used ZB as a vehicle to illustrate ideas and show possibilities.

The thoughts presented in *Alchemy of Touch* are part of a developing story designed to open new possibilities and insights to foster deeper understanding and change in how we approach well-being and healing. As the saying goes, "If we keep doing what we are doing, we will keep getting what we are getting." And, in view of our possibilities, what we are presently getting in terms of health, healing, and happiness is far short of potential. We need new, more effective ways of approaching personal actualization and world healing. It is my fondest wish that *Alchemy of Touch* might help foster that change.

Chapter One

Openings

One of my greatest curiosities in life has been about touch. What is it? How can we use it? What are its implications? And what are we touching when we touch another being?

Both my parents were very loving towards me, and always touched me appropriately. I was never hit. I was never spanked. I have no recollection of any negative experience around touch.

Although my parents were two beautiful people, they had very different worldviews. They lived in a time when problems were suppressed rather than discussed. These unresolved differences caused tremendous undercurrents of tension between them and in the household.

Because of this I became very sensitive to the unspoken world. I developed good intuitive skills. I knew when the room was tense, I knew when it was not tense, I knew when it was nice to be there, and when it was not nice to be there. I became very sensitive to the unseen world of energy and vibration.

I was the second of three children, and was a wanted child. My father was a chiropractor and my earliest information about touch came from him. Through his training he had developed high-level tactile skills and his touch always felt especially right and good. Whenever we got hurt as kids we would go to him to be "fixed" and he would make some gentle manipulation which always seemed to work. Thus my earliest experience of being touched was a response to his deft skills and I had a good deal of non-verbal input in this way. I think that to this day the very foundations of my understanding of touch and Zero Balancing stem from these early impressions. To give perspective to the quality of my father's work, I want to mention that when he was ninety years old, he was recognized as the oldest practicing chiropractor in the United States. He practiced until he was 93 and after he died was honored as chiropractor of the century.

I had several strategies as a child. One was to be good. I found that if I was good it created quiet surroundings and smoothed out tense environmental fields. A second strategy was to be sociable. My older brother was very smart. His relationship strategy in the family was intelligence and from my viewpoint he had a corner in that department. As I grew up, I did not want to be competitive with him, so I took the social route rather than that of the intellect. I relied more on my right brain than the left. Even my favorite doll as a child reflected the role I adopted in those days—the doll was Dopey from Snow White and the Seven Dwarfs.

Since I was very social, and believed by then I wasn't very smart, the academic side of school proved a very difficult experience. I struggled a lot but did do well enough to get into medical school. I choose an osteopathic college rather than an allopathic university because I wanted to have an education in manipulation as well as medicine.

I loved osteopathic school and for the first time I really enjoyed studying. This was a totally new experience for me and I came into my own as I immersed myself in learning. I didn't look to the right or the left. I had usually been in the bottom third of a class, but here I excelled. I completed the four years in medical school and graduated third in my class.

After graduation I completed an internship, and was accepted for a three-year internal medicine residency. After the first year of residence I realized I was moving away from the field of touch and manipulation, rather than closer to it. I left the program to enter into private practice.

At thirty, I realized that I had really devoted my life's energy to education, and had little true-life experience. I had totally identified with the image of being a doctor, and beneath that, I had no idea who I was.

I was not aware of the narrowness of my identity until my first marriage. It was a wake-up call, and I began to realize how limited and concretized I was. The marriage ended after three years, and I started searching for myself.

I began studying at the Esalen Institute, one of the first humanistic growth centers, located at Big Sur in Northern California. I went there in the late sixties, under the guise of becoming a better doctor. That was my excuse for going, but my real, albeit largely unconscious, purpose for going was to discover who I was beneath my identification as a doctor. I had amazing experiences there, and went over many edges. They changed my life. Gradually I began to let go of my limited self-identity. I let my buzz haircut grow out, grew a beard, stopped wearing a white coat in the office, and became more human.

While at Esalen I was introduced to Ida Rolf, the founder of Structural Integration. I studied with her and became a Rolfer. Several experiences I had in her training were to become linchpins to my understanding of how energy and structure work in the body.

A few weeks into the training I had the good fortune to be Ida Rolf's model for the last seven hours of a ten-hour protocol. Rolfing in those days was known to be painful, and as students we were hurting each other; all of us suffered our share of agony. One of my key experiences was that when Ida worked with me it didn't hurt. I was amazed. I remember feeling the deep pressure of her hands or elbow, but never felt pain itself. This was very confusing because other Rolfers, not only students, caused pain, often quite severe pain, doing what we thought she was doing.

In the following years, as I learned more about energy as a specific force or field in the body, I came to believe that Ida was actually working with energy as well as structure, although she was teaching us structure only. I am not sure how aware she was of energy concepts at that time. This was in 1971, before President Nixon had opened China to the West, before acupuncture was really known in the United States, and before energy was a household word. In retrospect, perhaps she may not have had the vocabulary to teach what I believe she was doing.

My view now is that she proprioceptively engaged energy in front of her physical structure, using her hands or her elbow. Then as she performed a physical motion, the energy preceded her physical form and "opened" the client's tissue microseconds before she made physical contact. This leading energy movement dispersed the tension in the field and released the obstruction that could have caused physical pain.

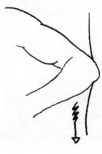

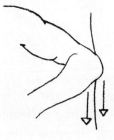

Physical connection only
Experience: Pressure with pain

Physical and energy connection
Experience: Pressure without pain

Another formative experience came during the fourth hour of the protocol when Dr. Rolf was working on my lower abdomen and had her elbow deep in my groin, heading south. I was apprehensive. At that moment her secretary called into the room, informing Dr. Rolf that her plane flight had been changed. The two women began a dialogue to rearrange her plans. Ida did not stop her work nor let up on the pressure of her elbow into my abdomen. For a moment I became even more apprehensive because of the delicacy of her position on my body and her possible distraction from where she was, or what she was doing. But as the conversation continued I surprisingly began to relax because I realized that she had not forgotten me and knew exactly what she was doing. She had not diverted attention from me or her elbow, despite the ongoing conversation.

This experience taught me a lot about "split-level consciousness." Split-level consciousness is a situation where we are doing two unrelated things at the same time, without sacrificing the experience of either. The consciousness is split into two places. We are all familiar with this state, although we may not identify it in so many words. Specifically how often do you drive home from somewhere and suddenly realize you are pulling into your driveway, and have no recollection of the trip? Clearly, part of you was paying attention to the road and the traffic even though you don't recall it. But your mind was thinking about other things. In a sense you were doing two unrelated things at the same time.

Another of my major learning experiences during the Rolf training came during the seventh hour of the protocol, when Dr. Rolf was working on my face and head. I had sustained a double skull fracture in a bicycle accident when I was eleven years old, and during that session Ida touched the affected areas with her hands. This set a whole recall process in motion, which I will report on more fully at a later point in the discussion of tissue-held memory.

I learned a great deal from Dr. Rolf and her training, and am very glad that I did it. Yet despite the importance of the training for me, Rolfing didn't become my personal expression, and I never became an active Rolfer.

About a year after my work with Ida Rolf, Professor J.R. Worsley, often referred to affectionately as JR, arrived at Esalen from England to teach acupuncture. One of the Esalen staff had been treated by Worsley while traveling in England, and had experienced such remarkable relief from a migraine headache that he had invited the doctor to present a program at Esalen. It all happened so quickly that Esalen did not have time to advertise his workshop schedule. They started calling people to fill the class. I was one of the people they called — and how fortunate for me! That week spent with Professor Worsley totally changed my life. On the basis of that experienced I decided to study with him in the UK, an undertaking that evolved into a ten-year project. I saw things during that first encounter which seemed unbelievable and which I could not begin to explain or account for from the perspective of my medical training. Professor Worsley showed us things that actually cracked my medical belief system. I suddenly realized there was much more to health than I had been taught in medical school or that I had understood in my own practice.

I was in Professor Worsley's first American class in England and completed the class the following year, receiving my United Kingdom License in Acupuncture. Although I had been trained and had seen the results from the sessions, deep down I still didn't believe that acupuncture worked. It was so contrary and foreign to my medical training that I was still in disbelief.

I had been gone from my medical practice for over two months. I was out of money and had a two-month backlog of patients — mostly for osteopathic manipulation. I desperately needed to work. On the second day home, I was in a car accident and fractured my right index finger in a number of places. My hand and lower arm were placed in a plaster cast, which prohibited me from doing any manipulation.

Although I could not do any hands-on osteopathic work, I found that I could hold an acupuncture needle. For two months, as my own injury healed, I did acupuncture on everybody. I started out that first day doing acupuncture on twenty patients. It was a baptism by fire.

To my amazement, people started to get well. I could not believe it. A number of these people were long-standing patients of mine and their chronic complaints were improving. As a result of these improvements, I was becoming an acupuncture convert. As I began to accept acupuncture, I went through a period of depression. I thought that I had wasted my life up until then. I had begun to think that the whole biomedical–osteopathic world had no value, that my education was useless, and that everything that mattered was in the needle.

It took a number of months for reality to dawn. During that time I experienced enough situations where acupuncture didn't help and where body handling proved a more satisfactory therapy to realize that no one therapy held all the answers. Yet, in the end, because I found acupuncture and bodywork to be so synergistically effective, I gave up the medical portion of my practice as a general family physician. From that time on, I stepped out of the medical world, dropped off the hospital staff, and became an independent practitioner. I devoted myself to acupuncture and manipulation, and eventually to acupuncture and Zero Balancing.

During my training in England, I had shared housing with a doctor from California. After the initial training with JR, we went back to the States for three months, after which we convened again in England. When I saw my roommate again, I realized that something fundamental had happened to him since we last met. His eyes were diamond clear, as if a veil had lifted. He was a very different person. I asked him what he had been doing, and he told me that he had been in India, where he had seen an Indian holy man, called Bhagawan Sri Sathya Sai Baba. It was while meditating under Sai Baba that he had developed this inner clarity. The difference in him was so remarkable, so outstanding, that I remember saying to myself: "Whatever that is, I want some!"

Such was my first awakening to the spirituality of the Eastern world. When I went home, I found that Transcendental Meditation was available in California. My wife Betty and I were given our mantras and we began meditating Maharishi–style. It was a wonderful, quieting experience.

A few months later, another Indian holy man, Swami Muktananda, came through Santa Cruz, and actually held darshan at my brother-in-law's house. "Darshan" means "to pay respect." I had never heard of this man, but I realized that maybe I did not have to go to India to meet a holy man. I was very curious and decided to attend the darshan. And as so many of us do, I asked to receive a sign: "Is this the right place for me to be? Is this the right thing to do? Is this for me? Give me a sign."

It was a strange but impactful afternoon. This was my first darshan. The procedure was to approach Muktananda, who was sitting in a chair, and bow down to him. To bow down to another human being was totally contrary to all my early Episcopal training. It seemed wrong, improper, and bizarre. Thus it was only through an act of will that I did this. I forced my body to bow before Muktananda.

Muktananda had a tradition of receiving hats from people. He would wear them and then give them to someone in the audience. I had gone up to him, bowed for darshan, and he had tapped me on the shoulder with a peacock feather. As I got up to leave, he called me back and put the hat he was wearing on my head. I went back and sat down, feeling a bit dazed and light headed. I remained altered, deeply quiet and calm, throughout the rest of the day. The only hat he gave that day was to me. I took this as the sign I had asked for.

I began studying and doing darshan with Muktananda. He held weekend programs around California. In those early days there would be around two hundred people at these gatherings. We would chant, meditate, and listen to talks and share experiences. The chants were all in Sanskrit, which was at first difficult but immediately engaging. Men and women were separated by a dividing isle and chanted alternate verses. Even though I didn't know the exact translation of the chants, they produced internal feelings of peace, sweetness, and camaraderie. I felt like I was coming home to something familiar.

Many of the meditations in those early days contained events that seemed very strange, and, contrary to the chanting, pushed a number of my reality buttons. Everyone sat on the floor, mostly on meditation cushions, with the men and women separated, as they were in all sessions. The lights would go down. At first things would be very quiet in the room but shortly into the meditation people would begin having spontaneous jerking movements of energy and emit involuntary sounds. You would hear deep sonorous rhythmic breathing, followed by occasional hooting and howling. Little by little more and more people began making sounds like animals, and soon the room sounded like an enlivened zoo. Many times, in those early days, I would think, "Fritz, what are you doing here?" If a psychiatrist had walked into the room, he would have wanted to commit everybody.

But at the end of a two-day retreat, I would feel especially good—open, free, wonderful. I kept on going back to the retreats whenever I could. Muktananda was known for shaktipat. Shaktipat means "energy transmitted to another." This could set in motion feelings of peace, the opening of channels in the body, or expanded meditative experiences. Whereas I had a number of experiences in meditation, my conservative midwestern upbringing prohibited me from making sounds of any sort, let alone animal sounds. Yet despite all the strangeness, I felt I had come home.

Several years later, Muktananda had a heart attack. Although he recovered, I realized that if I wanted to spend time with him, I had better do it now, because who knew how long he would be here? I heard he was giving a month's retreat in Northern California. I had a very busy practice in those days and found it difficult to get away for any extended periods but I felt called to go for a week.

That week was another life-changing event. There were about five hundred people at the retreat, and darshan was held in the gym of a college. On my last day a woman asked me if I would give her a ride to the airport. I agreed to this, and so had a specific time commitment to fulfill. I knew I had to leave the morning darshan at 10 AM, in the middle of the chanting. I made sure to sit on the aisle and placed my shoes at the back of the aisle so that I could find them easily and leave without disturbing others.

We were chanting "Govinda," which is one of the most beautiful chants, and halfway through it was time to go. From where I was sitting I bowed to Muktananda (which by this time was easy and joyful), got up, and went to where my shoes were. I was in the aisle, and Muktananda was sitting about one hundred feet apart from me exactly at the other end of the aisle. I had my shoes on, and turned to bow to him one more time. Suddenly, as I did this, a bolt of lightning shot across the room from him to me, and hit me on the top of the head! I was totally stunned. I jerked up in a daze, not expecting anything like this. I then realized that it was a very auspicious moment, so I bowed down again, and a second bolt of shakti came, about half as strong as the first. To this day, I can still see, and feel, that first bolt which I estimate was a hundred feet long.

I got up, dazed and shaken. I looked at my watch and saw I was already running late. The next two hours were taken up with driving the car, and rushing to get the woman to her plane. This was actually fortunate, because it prevented me from thinking about and analyzing what had happened.

Those hits of energy set in process an extraordinary period in my life. I got home and strange things began to happen. The first night home I remember waking up at three in the morning in a profuse cold sweat. I opened my eyes, and the room was filled with strange beings wearing brown monks' robes, with cadaverous faces. I was very frightened. I said out loud to myself and to them, "I am protected by God, and I am immune to outside influences." They disappeared. I do not know who they were, or why they were there, but I lay there for the rest of the night sweating and in panic. They had been real.

The next day, whenever I stood still, I could feel the earth begin to quake about a quarter of a mile into the earth; an earthquake beneath my feet. I was afraid the earth was going to open, cause great damage, and swallow me up. I found that if I did not stand still, this would not happen, so I kept moving. Whenever I stopped the earth would quake; I feared I would cause a major earthquake. This continued for two weeks and I became exhausted with fear and continued walking. Interestingly, when I was at work I was all right. I cooled down in some way. But in my own personal time earth tremors would happen.

We had a hot tub in the woods. We had walked its path thousands of times, as had many people. We had never found any glass on the path. That week, however, as I was walking, I kept finding pieces of glass. I'd walk along, and come across glass. I had never found glass before and I have never found glass since. I think I gathered about half a jar full. It was colored. My left-brain said, "I don't know where this is coming from!" But my right brain said, "You're materializing glass! So much energy is going through you, that when it hits the sand, it's galvanizing into glass."

When I went down to the hot tub and took the tub lid off, I would look into the water and it would start to have waves and then begin to boil. I would look away, only peeking back out of the corner of my eyes, and it would go quiet. I would turn to look at it full on, and it would start to churn again.

Again, my left-brain did not know what was happening. My right brain said, "This energy is flowing though you and out your eyes, and when it hits the water it churns." I was dismayed, fascinated, and fearful.

One night, I was lying in bed with my legs stretched out straight. It was about three in the morning, and I heard a dog bark. It must have been two miles away. I was listening, and I crossed my legs for comfort. The dog stopped barking. I uncrossed my legs, and the dog began barking again. For an hour and a half, that dog and I played as I crossed and uncrossed my legs. I am sure that I had a field of energy going through me that the dog was in touch with. When the field was open, he barked, and when I stopped the field by crossing my legs, he stopped.

During this time I was losing weight, sweating much of the time, was extremely frightened, and really felt I was going crazy. I had no one to talk to about these occurrences and nowhere to get a reality check. I did not know who could help. I became more and more panicky and frightened. I felt way off center and very alone.

One afternoon, about two weeks into this, I thought, "I've got to do something or I'm going to have a nervous breakdown." I could only think of three people in the world who might be able to help me. I got to the phone, and rang the first person. His answering machine said he was out of town for a couple of weeks. I called the second person; the line was busy. I was so desperate that I felt I could not even wait for him to finish his call. The third person was Muktananda himself.

I had the phone number of the retreat center where he was still supposed to be. I called and, after a number of rings, a woman answered the phone. Her voice was hesitant and timorous. I guessed that she was an inexperienced temporary volunteer probably about fifteen or sixteen years old. I suddenly felt very insecure that she could be of any help.

I put on my most formal persona, and said, "This is Dr. Smith in California. I was just at your retreat and I need to speak with Muktananda. I think I'm going insane. " She said, "I'm sorry, Baba is not available." I tried again. "Look I am a doctor and this is a medical emergency. I must speak with Muktananda." "I'm sorry." I tried to persuade her several more times, becoming more desperate by the moment. I thought my only hope of sanity was slipping away. After yet another attempt to get this girl to understand the seriousness of my plight, she unexpectedly asked, "Have you said your mantra?" I was so frustrated and angry that, without really thinking about it and just to humor her, I said, "Guru Om."

The moment I pronounced my personal mantra, "Guru Om," everything stopped. I was suddenly normal. It was like turning off a television set. I sat there on the edge of the bed, dazed. I couldn't believe it. I felt perfectly normal, as if nothing had ever happened. I hung up the phone without saying a word, and soon began to cry out of a sense of relief. To this day one of the strangest things about this whole experience was how completely and abruptly my weird experiences stopped — *after saying two simple words.* Two words that were said only half-heartedly to humor a young girl on the phone. The experience of those two weeks had been so real and all consuming, and then they simply stopped.

Many times since then I have thought that if I had the chance to live my life over again, I would do it differently. I wish I had not said the mantra. I would rather that someone had counseled me through the radical energy experience or that I had let nature resolve it in its own way. Of course that is easy to say now from a sane safe place. But I do know that even though I have lost the experience on a cognitive level, the process—whatever that was—has continued on an unconscious level of my being.

There were a number of offshoots from this experience of shaktipat. One was that my memory has never quite been as good as it was before the experience. Another was that it left me with a very quiet mind, for which I'm thankful. When I am not using my mind, it is quiet. I have very little background chatter, very little jabbering "monkey mind." It is said that the mind is a wonderful servant and a horrible master. For the most part since that event, my mind is the servant.

A third thing that happened was that my vision went blurry. I developed a kind of haze over my eyes that seemed like cataracts. I went to an ophthalmologist and she could find nothing wrong. A year later, I was back in India to see Muktananda at his ashram outside Bombay and had a consultation with Professor Jain, his translator and assistant. He listened to my story, looked at my eyes, and assured me that the haze would pass. About a year later I woke one morning and my eyes were clear.

During those heightened two weeks another event occurred which had probably the most significant far-reaching effect. One night I was in the hot tub. Our tub was big enough to stand comfortably within it, the water coming up to shoulder level. I could do a kind of a dervish movement without touching the sides. On that particular night I was slowly turning in the tub when all of a sudden it seemed like the top of my head opened. For perhaps one minute it felt as if there were a funnel in the top of my head, with new information just pouring in. This information was all about energy and its relationship to structure. It was about vibration, and how vibration and structure interrelate and interact in the human body.

My mind seemed like an old clock where all the springs and gears suddenly disengaged and then reassembled with new information and understanding. From that day on, I have known how energy and structure work together in the body, and how the particle and the wave relate within us. In a sense, Zero Balancing came from that experience and was born that night. Thirty years later I am still recalling information from the massive transmission I received at that time.

Over the years, as I have developed and taught Zero Balancing, I have been excited to see that the information of the transmission can be passed on to others. With training, other people can do ZB sessions as successfully as I can. If I were the only person who could do Zero Balancing, I would not be teaching it. The fact of the matter is that other people are now doing transformative treatments. The information for doing Zero Balancing is transmittable.

With the passage of time I have often wondered, "Are these experiences for real? Am I making these up? Did all this really happen in the way I recall?" My strong scientific background has forced me to question these events. Although my left-brain still has some questions, my deeper self knows this has all been real.

Another such experience happened in the 1980s when nine of us did a twenty-day trek in Nepal, around Annapurna Mountain. It was a wonderful yet rigorous trip. We climbed over one mountain pass at 17,850 feet. The physical and psychological demands of the trek often pushed us beyond our familiar limits and into expanded, altered states of consciousness.

I remember waking up one night in my tent. It was pitch black, but to my amazement I realized there was a lighted image hovering in front of my forehead. I could literally see a picture, as though a camera were projecting it onto a screen in front of me. There seemed an orifice in my forehead, and I could look through it and see things. I thought, "Fritz, you're making things up. You're dreaming. This isn't true." But it was real. For over an hour I experimented with the phenomenon. If I focused close in, I could actually see the walls and lining of the orifice itself in my forehead. If I looked through it, I could see scenes in front of my forehead, pictures projected into space. I could see into the past and I could see into the future. It was amazing. My third eye was open.

The experience of such an extraordinary phenomenon again shook my core, and made me question my perception of reality. I was reminded of the experiences I had with Muktananda many years before. My experience that night during the trek was another proof to me that the unseen body — in this case the sixth chakra or the third eye of the energy body — is not a figment of the imagination; it is quite literally real.

In 1998 a group of us did a silent trek in the desert of Morocco. The week culminated with a solitary 24-hour experience in the sand dunes, during which we were out of visual and auditory contact with each other. The following day I had an experience of Samadhi, that meditative state in which all distinctions between self and other are completely dissolved. That desert experience was an unexpected natural phenomenon and was one of my deepest experiences of bliss, another event that convinced me of the reality of vibration and the subtle body. It also showed me characteristics of how to work with energy. Nature again proved to be a great teacher. I will relate this story in depth in Chapter 12, when I write about expanded states of consciousness.

I have had many teachings. Some came from nature, life, and extra-ordinary experience; some from formal teachers, books, and school; some from years of private medical practice; and some from personal relationships. My relationship with Aminah Raheem has not only been special in its own right but very important in my development of ZB. Aminah Raheem is a transpersonal psychologist, author of *Soul Return,* and founder of the holistic hands-on health system, *Process Acupressure.* She is the mother of four children and has seven grandchildren.

When I first met Aminah, we were in many ways walking a similar path of health and healing, and the same path of spiritual quest. Our mutual exploration of healing led to colleagueship, then friendship, and then relationship. We married in 1992. Her influence and our many shared experiences have deeply affected my views — both our views — of healing.

We had left traditional perspectives many years prior to our first meeting. Aminah had moved from traditional to transpersonal psychology. I had moved from Western medicine to acupuncture and alternative health care. When we met some of our perspectives were very different. With her psychological background, Aminah searched for causes of problems. With my osteopathic/medical background, I sought to fix problems. Aminah's study with Arny Mindell influenced her to want to consciously process all of a person's traumatic events. My understanding of the relationship of energy to structure in the body led me to want to resolve problems directly without processing content. Our many discussions and experiences have led Aminah to process less, and me to process more. Even though our works — Zero Balancing and Process Acupressure — were created before we met, they have evolved significantly as a result of our partnership.

Aminah and I have had a similar spiritual quest. We were introduced to Bhagawan Sri Sathya Sai Baba at the same time in 1989. By that time Swami Muktananda had died, as had Aminah's spiritual teacher, Mohammad Subuh, founder of Subud. Although we weren't actually looking, both of us were open to a living spiritual teacher. We were studying together at a workshop with Graham Farrant, a world-class prenatal psychiatrist. He was a devotee of Sai Baba and a man so electric that just being in his field heightened one's joy and curiosity.

One evening after the class he showed a video of Sai Baba. Later at dinner Farrant offered us vibhuti (sacred ash) and then offered us amrita (sacred nectar), which he had brought with him from India. Though I do not know which of these was the catalyst — the vibhuti, the amrita, the video of Sai Baba, or Farrant himself — that night both Aminah and I had separate inner experiences of Sai Baba. Synchronicities began to happen, and within two weeks, we were both invited to present our work at a holistic health conference the following year in Bangalore, India, which included the opportunity to journey to Puttaparthi and actually do darshan with Sai Baba. When we met Sai Baba face-to-face our lives again changed radically.

Since then we have visited India a number of times and still have Sai Baba as our spiritual teacher and guide. It seems that there is energy in front of me opening the way, day-by-day. I am reminded of Ida Rolf's elbow opening my energy body to myself. It is an amazing thing. Though I work very hard, it feels effortless. Sai Baba has helped turn work into service, and that has changed the significance of my life.

This brief verbal passage through the moving moments of my life was meant to provide a perspective for the ideas I am about to present, and in particular to establish a foundation for a deeper exploration of touch and healing and an understanding of the potential of alchemical touch.

Let us begin ...

Chapter Two

Zero Balancing Session with Carl

Fritz: Hello, Carl. I'm looking forward to doing a Zero Balancing session with you. Is there's anything particular you wish us to address?

Carl: Yes. I always keep myself very busy and, in doing so, distance myself from my inner world. I think I'm now ready to come back into myself. In a sense I would like to "come home" and claim myself. Physically it feels that I need to fully occupy my body. As I think about that a lot of fear arises and I identify with our discussion yesterday regarding ancestral fear. There is strong refugee blood in my family from my Jewish, Austro-Hungarian, and German ancestry.

All the time they had to have their bags packed and be ready to go on a moment's notice. There was always an undercurrent of fear, uncertainty, and a pervasive refugee mentality. Whatever this fear is in me, it makes me feel I can't express myself. The sensation I have is being a squeezed like tube of toothpaste. It's up here *(Carl indicates his head)* and it can't come out. It affects just about every aspect of my life and, at this moment, I am ready to look at it more deeply.

But all that seems to have been paled by a dream that I had last night, that I'd like to bring into this session.

Fritz: What was that dream?

Carl: In the dream, Fritz, you were the giver. You were looking at me while putting a fulcrum into my feet. And I was watching your eyes which were incredibly intense. You said to me, "I'm getting some readout about your family. Do you have a relationship with your grandparents?" I said I had a relationship with my grandmothers, because they were still around but not my grandfathers, because they were dead. Then you said: "Think about your grandfathers." Here there was an image of two square chimneys, one with a square metal covering that was neatly finished and the other was still showing cement, and not properly finished.

At that point I got up and went into a room. In that room I thought about my paternal grandfather, whom I only met once. He was a very powerful figure but there didn't seem to be anything in that image of him that I could connect with. Then I began to think of my maternal grandfather. And I ... *(pause)* ... I started to rage, and really shout and pound. He's never been part of my life ever, nor part of my consciousness. He died when I was seventeen. He was a very big, overpowering, pasty, invasive figure who used to give us jellies in the house. He lived in this huge house in Hampstead and I felt very uncomfortable in that house, always.

When we moved over from Zimbabwe, we lived in that house for some time; I don't know how long it was. So, in the dream I was raging away in a way I had never raged before. I was raging from my stomach and my throat was clear. I was holding onto this chimney and I was pounding the chimney without the metal top. Yet, this man has never actually been part of my waking consciousness at all. When he died, I didn't feel anything. My only recollection surrounding his death was that I was alarmed that nobody really felt anything.

Fritz: You knew him though?

Carl: I knew him, yes. But I didn't like being in his presence. He made me feel very uncomfortable. So, before I woke up from the dream, you and a group of people, I can't remember exactly who, came into the room and saw me pounding the chimney. That's when I woke up, with my heart pounding, like it would explode. I was weeping, my whole lower body was cramping.

It seemed to be an alarming response to something that was really rather frightening. You were very much there in my consciousness. Sharing the dream with everybody here was also a prospect of real terror, because it was like ... I don't know what it was like. It was just that the dream came out of nowhere. That's frightening. The space I need to go into is a space I have never been to before. I feel I really need to trust before I get to that space. It will probably be quite a suggestible state to be in.

Fritz: We will all honor that.

Carl *(smiling and looking around at the group):* I really need some reality checks around me. All this has just completely come out of the blue.

Fritz: I'm not a dream analyst and I don't believe we or you need to figure out the dream. Just let things flow through you. Let things stay in motion. I believe that you — that all of us — are in motion in a very important way — possibly stimulated by things that happened here yesterday, and the day before. We have all been very intense and focused these past few days, and are in a very high, connected field.

Carl: Yes. Last night, we were talking about leaving the body and having out of body experiences, and all that kind of stuff. It feels like something I've done a lot in my life and that I've been very good at doing. It's been my response to feeling unsafe.

I thought about my grandfather coming home from work and my grandmother waiting on him all the time. Everyone would lay a carpet out for this man. I remember feeling: "This is disgusting, there is something that is really not ringing true here." When I thought about my grandfather last night, I got out of bed and wrote all this down. I wanted to remember the dream exactly as it was. I wanted it to be authentic and not take hours and days of processing and rethinking. When I switched the light off I just had this almighty sense of beating him to pulp. And I slept like a baby afterwards. It was a great dream.

Fritz: Wow. What an important dream. The deep rage you felt, and the things you didn't feel when you were around him, were released. You beat him to a pulp. You released this deeply held stuff you had as a kid; you just let it come out. You've got it, you are not disempowered, you've got your inner strength, like show me the next guy, huh!

Laughter

You let the inner rage go. Good for you. It's good work. It's hard to let rage go if it's so deeply buried. My guess is that you are more vulnerable at this moment, not from just telling us your dream, but because you opened some deeper passage within yourself.

Pause

Is there anything else you would like to share or things you would like to frame for the session? We have plenty to do but I want to be sure that there are not other specifics you would like to address.

Carl: I think that pretty much runs through all the things that I can think of at the moment.

Fritz: If something else comes up, let me know.

I'd like to go back and say a few things before we work. You mentioned carrying the ancestral fears of refugees. Do you think you are serving your ancestors or your lineage by carrying these?

Carl: No.

Fritz: Do you think you could serve your lineage better if you worked these issues out now and therefore, not give them to your kids to carry forward?

Carl takes a sharp in breath and breathes out quickly.

Carl: Oh yes.

Fritz: This ancestral line, wherever you picked it up, is a movement going through you and potentially to future generations. I believe we can affect what ancestral imprinting we pass on. First, we need to know that we do carry imprinting and, second, we need to know that we have the ability to affect it. Much of our heritage is time honored and true, and is important to pass on to our children, and our children's children. But there are things we would rather not pass on. Some imprints carry too much shadow, others are outmoded for this or the next century. To the extent we feel we are not breaking a spoken or unspoken commitment or a contract with our ancestors, we have an opportunity — perhaps a responsibility — to unburden ourselves, our ancestors, and our future generations. With your permission I will look for these areas of imprinting and help you reprogram them.

Carl: I'd be very happy if you did that. I give you my permission.

Fritz: You don't see any disrespect in doing that? You don't see any problems if we were able to release some of the imprinting? I want permission for working on this level so we don't create karma from the work.

Carl: *(pause)* No. I think we have gotten what we can from them.

Fritz: I want to highlight your statement of "wanting to come home" as part of my strategy for the session. You indicated you are living up here *(Fritz indicates Carl's head)* and you want to get down here *(Fritz indicates Carl's middle)*. This makes sense. The *dan tien*, our center of power, is located in the pelvis. Our energetic "home."

This reminds me of instructions given to singers: "If you reach for a high note *(Fritz makes a sound from his throat as if he's about to lose his voice)*, find it in the pelvis." Go deep into yourself where the energy lies, not to the head. If you have feelings of wanting to "move up," I suggest that you direct them downward into the pelvis, into the *dan tien*. Keep going deep and you'll find that your creativity will naturally arise.

"I want to come home" could mean different things. From the tenor of our conversation I can interpret your remark to mean "come home to who I really am." ZB can offer you the experience of coming home, not just in the pelvis in the physical sense, but in the greater sense of who you actually are.

Exactly how the strategies will manifest or be accomplished will depend on what I find in the course of the ZB. So, if you are ready, let's begin and see where it takes us.

Carl: Okay. And thanks.

Fritz moves behind Carl to begin evaluation of the shoulder and pelvic girdles, which is carried out without further comment. Carl then lies down and Fritz goes to his feet, and does a half moon fulcrum through the legs.

Fritz (to everyone): My basic instruction for the person on the table is to just relax and enjoy the session. I want as little of their mental engagement as possible. To the extent that the person is in their left brain, thinking or tracking the session, the working signs are blocked.

Fritz (to Carl): Just relax and enjoy yourself. You have nothing to do, just enjoy. Feel how good and safe it feels.

Fritz (to everyone): I want to introduce the idea or idiom of safety early in the session because to be safe limits fear.

Fritz (to Carl): I'd like you to experience safety.

Carl breathes out deeply.

Fritz (to everyone): We shared earlier about alchemical fulcrums, and how to build the vibration and the power of an individual fulcrum. We can also create an alchemical session. We enhance the vibration throughout the body and keep it contained so that the entire session becomes an alchemical event. The whole ZB becomes empowered, rather than just a single fulcrum. This will be of value here in that I plan to look for ancestral imprinting deep in his fabric.

Fritz begins to work more intensely on the front of the right side of Carl's pelvis.

Fritz: Just keep letting go.

Carl continues to relax into the session. Fritz works on the sacroiliac and lower back, and then sits on the side of the couch, placing Carl's right leg across his lap as he prepares to evaluate the hip joint.

Fritz (to the group, as he reaches with his second hand under the buttock): Although in my mind's eye I can almost see where Carl is holding energy, in Zero Balancing I need to actually locate that place in terms of touch. The advantage of knowing how to evaluate for held energy is that I don't have to guess or use intuitive sense to locate it. I will discover it as I systemically evaluate.

Fritz finishes evaluating the hips and moves down to the feet.

Fritz (to everyone): Carl has a clear, well-coordinated body. It is dense, in the best sense of the word, very full, and holds a lot of intellectual intensity. Up to this point I have checked the girdles, sacroiliac, dorsal hinge, lumbar spine, hips, and the feet and have not yet located significant held energy. I will now check the pubic symphysis. Perhaps it is there.

Fritz (to Carl): Carl, would you locate the top of your pubic synthesis for me?

Carl does so. Fritz places a finger on the superior pole of the pubis and connects with his second hand on Carl's right sacroiliac joint.

Fritz: Hmm. Right here there's a density. It's very old. It's very deep. I'm not hurting you, am I? *Carl shakes his head a little to indicate the pressure is fine.* Now, just open. *After a few seconds Fritz releases his fulcrums and stands back from the table. Carl sighs. Emotion is clearly bubbling through him. Fritz moves to place his hand over Carl's hands that are resting on his chest. Carl releases breath after breath.*

Fritz (pausing): Carl, I'd like you to set down the packed bags of the refugees, just set them down. You don't need to carry them any longer.

A wave of emotion seems to flow through Carl, he contorts his face in an effort to contain it and breathes out. It passes, dissipates, his face returns to an expression of inner watchfulness.

Fritz (continuing to address Carl): Any part of the ancestral vibration or imprinting you don't need to carry, set that down. *Carl lets go of a deep breath.* Carry a beautiful image of your ancestral history and keep that alive but set down the confused and discordant non-serving parts. And—very important—if any guilt arises as you do that, let it go as well. *Carl breathes out deeply twice more.*

Carl: It feels like something won't release from my back. *Fritz does a half moon fulcrum through the legs and then moves to the top of the table and slips his hands under Carl's upper back. Carl's body shudders as he releases further. He continues to breathe out deeply.*

Carl: I feel like I am just walking away from a train station full of refugees.

Fritz: Do it!

Carl repeatedly says: "God" ... "God" ... Carl is experiencing emotion too strong for him to answer otherwise. His eyes moisten and the power of the moment emanates out into the room, which everyone feels. Fritz continues to work on his upper back, the fluidity increases and the staccato movements in Carl's stomach subside. At one point Fritz comfortingly puts his hand over Carl's hands and whispers "I've got you" with deep caring in his voice. Carl takes the opportunity in between the waves to express in words what is going on.

Carl: The trouble is part of me wants to stay in the station.

Fritz: You can stay for a moment. *Carl breathes out again.*

Fritz (to everyone): I'm going to amplify the whole field for Carl, so there's more juice to work with. *Fritz puts both hands under Carl's shoulders, and lifts with a deep fulcrum under each hand. Renewed strength comes into Carl's expression.*

Carl: I'm giving myself permission to go. I don't want to feel like I'm running away.

Fritz: No, you're not running away. You're consciously walking away.

Carl: I feel sort of cowardly.

Fritz: No. You're walking towards something bigger and more important. *Carl continues to let go of his breath deeply and consciously. Fritz moves back down to check the pubis area. Receiving Carl's permission, he makes contact again with the pubic symphysis.*

Fritz: I can feel a difference. A big difference already. You're fine. Go slow. Keep coming down. Very good.

Fritz moves from the pubic area and goes down to the left foot, where he puts in another double ice cream scoop fulcrum. Carl shows various working signs, and for some time there is silence. Finally Fritz speaks to Carl.

Fritz: What's happening? *Carl smiles broadly.*

Carl: I've just chosen to sit in the sunlight.

Fritz: Good for you. *Carl looks relaxed. His face has a washed, fresh look.*

Fritz moves up once again to the top of the couch.

Fritz: I'm going to press quite firmly on your shoulders and direct your energy directly down into the pelvis. Feel it down there; experience it. Feel the energy moving downward into your pelvis and then keep it there for a moment. *Fritz continues to work directing the energy down to the pelvis, and at one point uses his knuckles to push down Carl's chest to help the flow. Suddenly Carl lets out another exclamation "God!"*

Fritz: Too much?

Carl: No, it's just such a relief.

Fritz: Keep letting go of anything extraneous. It's not yours. Focus on the energy in your pelvis. *(pause)* Good. Feel the experience that you've really come home; that you have found your center.

Carl's expression subtly changes from one of calm relaxation to a glowing look of someone who is finally at peace. He lets out a long, slow, and gentle breath, and suddenly another wave goes through the body; this time it looks almost as if he could burst into laughter at any moment.

Fritz: I'm getting ready to close. I'd like you to turn around and look back at the people in the railway station and wave good-bye. Sense your accomplishment, your strength, your individuality. Be sure there is no residual attachment.

Then turn and walk into your own future, free of the experiences that are no longer part of you. Appreciate a deep accomplishment—a true sense of freedom. And finally, re-focus on the energy in your pelvis, and establish yourself there.

Carl looks radiantly at peace.

Fritz (to everyone): It is like there is a little gyroscope deep in the pelvis. If we activate it, it keeps us stable and grounded; it keeps us functioning and powerful; it keeps us fluid and moving—not fixed, not stuck, not fearful.

Fritz places his hands on Carl's head and works with micro fulcrums over the scalp and then down onto the neck. The pleasure Carl experiences is tangible to the rest of the group. Everyone is smiling broadly, reflecting Carl's look of deep contentment.

Fritz: Before closing, is there anything else you want to let go of or re-program? I want to be sure you've accomplished everything you want.

Carl: One thing. I still feel that I can't disconnect from the fact that they are remaining at the station.

Fritz: It's their choice to be there.

Carl: Yes.

Fritz: Who knows the bigger picture? I don't think it's your responsibility to take them from the station. Feel that it's okay for them to be there for as long as they wish. Don't be trapped by that.

Carl: I don't have to feel guilty that I've the courage to go?

Fritz: Absolutely not. Guilt can be an archetypal reaction to change, because you're going against conditioning. This seems situational, archetypal and not personal guilt. But don't deny it. Feel it and then let it go. In a sense it isn't yours. *Carl breathes out again, and there is a hint of a giggle there.*

Fritz: Your responsibility is towards your future, not to your past. *Carl nods in acknowledgment. This thought clearly hits home.* To your family, your wife, your future.

Carl: I can see that.

He makes a sound that echoes his grasping of this truth.

Fritz: If you still have a question, look back at the station. See your ancestors waving good-bye to you.

Carl smiles from ear to ear.

Carl: I can now clearly see my path ahead.

Fritz: See — and feel — all your ancestors wishing you well. *(pause)*

Carl: Yes.

Fritz: Experience how good it feels to be here now. Imprint that feeling, how good it is to release the past. This is healing. One more piece. Let your inner child feel how good it feels for what you have done.

Carl's smile remains, but there is a delicate softness that is added on hearing these words.

Fritz: With all that has happened here, I want to turn to acupuncture and check Carl's pulses. I am curious to see how he is faring from this perspective following such a large session. If any element were lagging, I would support it. I'm very drawn to CV2, just above the pubic symphysis and, depending on the pulses, perhaps other points further upward on the conception vessel. There is no question that the channel is really open at this moment.

Deirdre offers some needles and Fritz, after asking Carl's permission, takes his pulses and proceeds to stimulate acupuncture points on Carl's legs, pubic area, and chest.

Fritz: Before taking the pulses, I had no idea which element, if any, might need help. The pulses indicated the earth element was staggering and welcomed assistance to digest the experience and to allow Carl to take it in to a very deep level.

Carl sits up. He looks radiant. He says just one word: "Wow" and bursts into a deep belly laugh, in which the group joins.

Carl: That's incredible.

Fritz: Remember, as you step off the table, you'll be stepping onto, and into, a different world. *Carl steps down onto the floor.* Look at how much taller he is!

We all laugh. Carl does indeed look tall, almost several feet taller, like a giant.

Fritz: Walk into your new world. Walk into your future.

Carl walks with a power and density unrecognizable from his pre-session amble. A natural grace is clearly evident. He giggles as he moves. (laughter)

Carl: It's just incredible. Wow. Wow. Wow. God. God. I feel so much lighter.

Fritz: When you're ready, go outside and have a walk, and keep feeling the lightness. Don't mentally figure out what's going on. Just experience the newness. Keep seeing yourself walking into the future, secure in your base. No matter what it is. Just keep walking into the future. Occasionally turn around and wave good-bye to your past, and see it waving back to you.

Carl: God. Incredible. It's incredible. It's just incredible. *(lots of laughter)* It is all very, very new, like I've got different muscles and —like I've been given new freedom.

Fritz: To formally close this session, give me a hug. *They hug.* You're now free of us and on your own. Enjoy.

Carl's walk was long and fulfilling. The room still retained an energy. It was evident that for the rest of the day there was more laughter and vibrancy than on previous days.

Carl's report of the ZB experience

Having had such a powerful dream last night, I was aware that I was carrying a tremendous amount of emotion. I still felt vulnerable and suggestible from the dream. I knew it would take a lot of trust for me to let go and get to a place in myself that I'd not been to before, or certainly not for a long time. Since first meeting Fritz and seeing him work, I have always been impressed by the clarity of his work and by his honest intention to free people to live with greater congruence and without dependence on him. With that trust it was just a matter of finding the courage inside myself to ask for what I needed. I didn't want to fabricate anything but equally I didn't want to avoid anything.

I felt wobbly when I first laid down, but very safe the moment Fritz touched my body. After he worked on my sacroiliac, pelvis, legs and feet, it was reassuring to hear that my body was in good shape. As soon as he placed his hands on my pubic bone I could feel the tightness, density, and rigidity of the area. It felt painful but it was good to feel the fulcrum. I felt a huge release of emotion downward into my lower body — just releasing unnamed and unknown stuff. It felt tender, vulnerable, and right at the center of my being. As he allowed those energies to release and suggested that I also set down all those vibrations that tie me to my ancestral past — the sense of always having my bags packed, always being on the move, of being a refugee — it felt overwhelming.

The session became like a waking dream. I immediately had the picture of standing on the platform of a train station — in the open air, in black and white, with a crowd of Jewish people in overcoats, with scarves or hats on their heads, carrying suitcases, baskets, bags, rucksacks. There was a hushed atmosphere of extreme and sustained fear. Of being the hunted, like a rabbit at the side of the road, breathing rapidly, staring wildly, helplessly. All you could hear was the breeze on the trees and the shuffle of feet. It was so desolate. How could I leave these people? How could I walk away from their pain and leave them there? How could I save myself knowing they were still there? And yet the relief of just putting my bags down on the platform was huge.

Fritz encouraged me to do more.

I kept walking to the fence gate, trying to leave. Everything was brutal and I felt selfish. I couldn't go — at least not without enormous guilt. Every time I reached the gate, I'd walk back into the center of the crowd of refugees. All their eyes were blank with fear, as if they had lost all control, or desire for control, in their lives.

Fritz asked what was going on. I told him I found it desperately painful to leave. I also remembered saying that the attachment to my ancestral past was not serving me any longer and wouldn't serve my own family.

Fritz acknowledged my feelings and encouraged me to find the courage to leave.

I know I have lots of courage, so I finally managed to open the gate. The click of the latch rang out across the whole platform. Everyone stared. I felt devastated and felt pulled back. But I also felt relieved without the weight of the bags.

On the other side of the gate was an arch created by a huge yew tree. It cast an enormous, cold shadow on the ground. Through the arch I could see a beautiful green pasture bathed in a golden light and warmed by the sun. It was pure Cotswold English countryside, gentle and comforting and full of color, if I could just get there. Under the yew tree it was cold. I was facing the refugees on the platform, picking out their coats through the railings of the fencing. I could only glance over my shoulder at the warmth through the yew.

Fritz said "Go on." I felt agony inside; I felt like there was a huge groaning. Fritz held me firmly under the shoulder blades and told me he had me. I was through into the sunlight. God it was beautiful. So warm. So safe. Such a relief.

When I faced toward the refugees, I felt like a coward, leaving them in their pain, not helping them to get out too. It was an act of will for me to turn my back on them and walk further away, deeper into the golden, early evening sun. I walked through a little church graveyard and sat on the grass on the other side. I could smell the grass and feel the energy in the ground.

Then Fritz suggested I look at all my ancestors waving me good-bye. It was a revelation to think that they may actually wish me well on my way. I pictured them all lined up by the fence. They were still in black and white, or certainly very grey, washed out colors. And, yes, there they were, waving. They were sad—a resigned sadness—but they were actually waving me on my way, not spitting hate, or chucking guilt at me. Wow!

I still felt a huge pull to go back—especially now they were being so nice to me! It was almost magnetic. I would experience the glow of the sun and the warmth of the ground, and then want to go back. What could I do to really be free?

Beyond me was a hill. If I could just walk over the hill, then the train platform would no longer be in sight. This was the last step. Fritz encouraged me by saying that the rest of my family had chosen to stay on the platform, that I wasn't responsible for them, and that I had chosen to leave. I turned to look at them again. They were still waving. A little tearful but I had the clear sense that they had chosen to be there. Perhaps because that was more closely their heritage, and they felt the need to stay in solidarity. It was not so closely mine, and I knew deep in me that this was not serving me, nor would it serve my new family.

And off I went.

Ahead was a long road, winding around rolling hills and stretching into the distance. The evening light played along the hillside. There was nothing else; just a wonderfully clear sense of my path, uncluttered, inviting, unknown. Having turned my back on my ancestral past, I felt a huge sense of relief, a lightness, a bounce in my feet and a thrill of excitement and strength in my body.

When Fritz asked me to enjoy the sensation and then to bring my inner child to the scene to share it, it was, quite simply, a moment of pure bliss. There is no other way to describe it. Complete congruence. I felt like Dick Whittington, with my arm around me as a little boy, beaming, excited, expectant, and ready to walk down the road. I'd let go of the baggage, and could live my life.

Chapter Three

Fundamentals

We live in one of the most exciting periods of history when Eastern understandings of energy, meditation, and healing are being validated and corroborated by Western science. It isn't that the East needs the scientific validation; rather that the West needs to believe that there is a meaningful reality in Eastern thinking. The world of Western medicine and health care is moving through a period of major change and chaos, struggling with patient demand for more holistic care. New values are coming into the consciousness of both health care providers and patients, partially fueled by Eastern influences.

The Alchemy of Touch arose out of this interplay between Eastern thinking and Western science. It explores different ways of approaching health and self help, of healing and self-healing. It is based on accepting the idea that energy is a real and specific force in the body and that its vibratory nature can be used as a healing tool. This chapter explores a model that integrates Eastern and Western ideas, and highlights the theory and practice of using touch to influence a person's vibratory nature.

Everything is Energy: A Need for Clear Terms

We need a specific definition of terms and images to have a meaningful dialogue regarding energy. For Zero Balancing, I choose to use the quantum physics model, which says that the particle and the wave represent two fundamental aspects that comprise our universe. Granted that the particle and the wave are both forms of energy, in Zero Balancing I reserve the word *energy* to represent the wave aspect. Specifically, I use the wave and particle to refer to two distinct "bodies" of the human being. I correlate the wave aspect of energy to the energy body and the particle aspect to the structural body.

This distinction becomes more usable as other words and ideas are added to distinguish qualities of wave and particle. For example, I see energy represented by words such as wave, vibration, movement, tension, and function. I see particles represented by words such as particle, structure, matter, mass, and form. These variables intersect and interface in myriad ways. Each way offers a different insight, consideration, and therapeutic potential.

Understanding particle and wave in terms of the body

The bodies of structure and energy are interdependent and in relationship, even though their anatomy, physiology, and pathophysiology are different. The anatomy of the physical body is fairly well agreed upon. We can see, feel and touch the body, and through surgery and dissection agree upon its structure. Many standard anatomical reference books have been written. However, the anatomy of the energy body is less tangible, more difficult to define, and less well agreed upon. Descriptions vary from culture to culture.

The energy body

The energy systems within the body have been defined in many ways: the acupuncture model, with meridians, acupoints, and in-depth descriptions of qi (energy); the chakra model, with seven primary and multiple secondary energy vortices; the yoga model, with nadis and the four bodies of physical, subtle, causal, and super causal; the quantum physics model with particle and wave; the holographic model, with intersecting of wave patterns; the Buckminster Fuller model of tensegrity and its related compressive and tensional forces; and many others. Each of these system descriptions has a reality, and many interrelate and inform one another.

In Zero Balancing, I prefer to step back and consider the energy anatomy from a more global viewpoint. I prefer to say that each person has one energy body, which is inclusive of the specific descriptions and experiences gleaned from various cultures over the centuries.

Energy physiology

The functions of the energy body allow for many things to be accomplished. One is to connect us to the greater whole of nature; another is to stabilize us as a functioning, somewhat independent eco-system; and a third is to provide us with a way to respond to moment-by-moment internal and external change.

The Universal Connection

All upright objects function as lightning rods, conducting currents of energy between sky and earth. In our bodies the skeletal system plays a key role in this regard. Along with the muscular system, it allows us to stand upright in the gravitational field. Whereas our whole body is involved in conducting these currents, the skeleton is our primary armature and main tissue involved. It is the densest tissue and therefore conducts the strongest of these currents. In the upright stationary position the skeleton allows us our greatest span, and therefore the greatest polarity, between the sky and the earth.

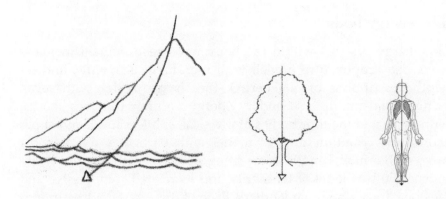

The universal connection.
All upright objects conduct currents of energy between heaven and earth.

The Individual Ecosystem

A second function of energy is to enable us to operate as an independent entity in the world. It provides each of us with an autonomous internal drive system. This internal system can be summarized in terms of three levels.

Internal system: first level

The deepest level of our internal energy system involves the skeleton and the pattern of movement engendered by walking. Every step stimulates compression, and a line of tension develops from the foot that is contacting the earth through the body's center of gravity into the opposite shoulder. As you step down onto your opposite foot another diagonal line is established from that foot through the center of gravity to the other shoulder. In normal walking these diagonal vectors are converted into a complicated figure-eight spiral pattern.

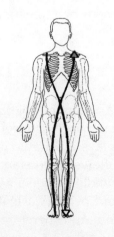

The deepest internal flow
is through the skeleton,
engendered by walking

Internal system: second level

The middle level of our internal energy system is the movement of energy through soft tissue. The best map of these pathways is described in classical Chinese acupuncture, which includes the twelve basic meridians, their deep pathways, their relationship to the organs of the body, and the eight extra meridians. These and other flows are well described in any number of texts of Chinese medicine and acupuncture.

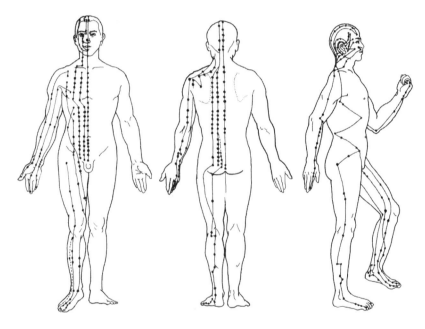

The channel pathways of Chinese acupuncture

Internal system: third level

The third level of energy is located just beneath the skin. It is an insulating energy, known as *wei qi,* and is described in detail, along with its pathways, in Chinese traditional medical texts. One function of energy is to give us an insulation or buffer that allows us to move into other vibratory or energetic fields and remain clearly at interface. *Wei qi* is a vibration, somewhat coarser than that which flows through the meridians. Vibrations constantly bombard us. The vibration of sound, for instance, strikes our eardrum and we hear a sound. But it also strikes and impacts on our entire body.

Much of the impact of these sound waves is reflected off the body by the density of the skin and the *wei qi* vibration. Have you ever felt irritated by loud music? If so, you can assume that part of the impact of the sound got through your layer of insulation and into your body. Or have you become irritated when standing in a strong wind? If so, the same reasoning applies.

Vibrations in the form of heat, cold, and other environmental forces are assaulting us every minute of the day. People with deficient *wei qi* tend to have weaker or poorly defined energetic boundaries. They tend to get sick more easily, may be oversensitive to external vibrations of any sort, or even be unfocused as a result of experiencing random psychic influences.

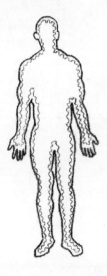

Wei Qi, the denser vibration just beneath the skin

The Background Field

The third basic factor of energetic physiology provides us with the ability to respond to moment-by-moment change. This is accomplished through the medium of the background energy field. The background field is that energy which can change vibratory rate in response to here and now events. The background field permeates our entire body and extends beyond the skin. It composes the auric field that surrounds us.

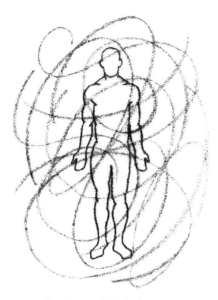

Background field of energy

To help further conceptualize the background field, consider the ocean. Water moves in complicated ways. Each water molecule has its own movement. Additionally, water moves in patterns, and these patterns of movement are within other patterns of movement. For instance, all molecules of water are involved in the rising and falling tides caused by the sun, moon, and planetary influences. Some molecules may be involved in the oceanic Gulf Stream drift or the Japanese current. If they drift toward the surface of the ocean they may crash against the shoreline as part of a wave. Or they may be in swirls and turbulence as it flows around or over large stationary rocks. Some molecules of water, however, do not form part of an organized pattern, or are not strongly held within another configuration, and are responsive to changes in the immediate environment.

In our bodies, the vibration of energy in the background field is somewhat similar to those uncommitted or marginally committed molecules of water. This is the vibration that responds to our moment-by-moment change and is a medium through which emotions can be experienced. It gives us a way to feel the vibration of anger, happiness, sadness, and so forth.

If we are in another person's auric field, we often experience their feelings or emotions as our background field begins to resonate with theirs. The background field allows us to be congruent with our situation and with the moment.

As in the ocean, the patterns of vibration in the body are complex. A person who is chronically depressed, for example, may have a background field that is generally flat, de-energized, and with lessened vitality. The person who is continually anxious has a field that reflects agitation. Within these general patterns, however, there is still a sensitivity that allows other emotions to emerge. The depressed person has times of happiness and the anxious person times of serenity. The background field is capable of being so sensitive and responsive that it can hold and show the infinite nuances of our experiences. Consider anger. It can be a sudden outburst of emotion; it can be cold or calculating, self-righteous, or perhaps suppressed into the field. All these nuances can be coordinated within the background field.

Distinguishing Structure and Energy

In this model, I perceive the human being comprised of particles and waves, represented by two bodies, one of structure and one of energy. These bodies have distinct identities yet operate in relationship.

Either body can be identified through touch. You can identify the body of structure by paying attention to the feel of the tissue beneath your fingers. You can identify the body of energy by paying attention to the movement involved in the part. This can be gross movement, or a micro-movement feeling such as buzzing or tingling. You can appreciate both bodies by keeping awareness on the feel of the structure under your fingers as you introduce a motion.

Through palpation you want to be able to distinguish the particle aspect of the body, the wave aspect and their combined presence. Once these distinctions are clear you can then work with the variables separately or in terms of their relationship. Many health issues resolve in a balanced coordination between energy and structure.

Internal body signals can help distinguish energy and structure. A wonderful teacher in this regard is the moving sidewalk found in many airports. Compare the difference of your own body sensations when you are walking on the floor and when you are walking on the moving sidewalk. When you walk on the solid floor it seems stable, secure, and ordinary. By contrast when walking on the moving surface it feels more alive, awake, and responsive. When I touch structure alone I have a static, solid feel; when I engage the energy body, I have the feeling that part of me is in motion, similar to the feelings I get when walking on a moving surface. My own body signals tell me when I have engaged the energy body.

Characteristics of energy and bone

Different tissues of the body have different energetic characteristics. These differences show us options of how to work with a person's structure and energy.

Bone of has a number of characteristics that give it a special place in relation to the energy body. Bone is the densest and most rugged of our body tissues. As noted, it is our physical armature and along with the muscle system it allows us to stand upright in the world in relation to gravitational fields. It supports, encloses, and protects vital organs, and in general helps support all tissues.

On the physical level, stimulation of bone causes further bone to form. Stress on bone is necessary to keep it healthy and responsive, although over time, too much or too little stimulation can be deleterious. Excess stress promotes the formation of bone spurs and arthritic changes, while lack of stress promotes bone absorption.

On the energetic level, bone is at the core of the energy body and, because of its density, conducts the strongest currents. The skeleton is involved in both the vertical flows of energy between heaven and earth, and the deepest currents flowing through our individual ecosystem. It transmits and conducts electrical, vibratory, and other energetic fields as well as mechanical forces such as compression and tension.

Bone has piezoelectric properties. Piezoelectricity is electricity produced by pressure and is one of the known bridges between the mechanical and energetic worlds. Pressure on bone initiates an electric current.

Bone is relatively stable in the body. It is designed to absorb the stress of movement and soft tissue attachments. It cannot "roll with the punch" of a great variety of stimuli as soft tissue does with its softer, yielding nature. Bone itself is a non-contractile tissue and can neither expand nor contract to absorb or deflect stimulation. Nor can it move out of the way of a force. In a sense bone stands naked and exposed before many stimuli.

Bone resonates with the vibration of impact. If a pillow is struck with a hammer, an initial thud of impact is heard but it has no lasting resonance. Cushioning material absorbs the force of impact. If a metal beam is hit in the same manner, it rings. The force of impact translates into vibration. The whole beam is set in resonance. Similarly when a bone is struck, as a hit on the shinbone, the impact is painful and involves the whole leg.

Characteristics of foundation and semi-foundation joints

Joints, articulations, and the ligaments that support joints are an integral part of the skeletal system. Some joints are primarily designed for movement and locomotion, while others are designed to give stability and transmit forces within the system. In the context of energy, we are particularly interested in the latter group of joints. They are referred to as the *foundation* and *semi-foundation* joints. The major foundation joints include the cranial bones of the skull, the sacroiliac joints, the intertarsal joints of the feet, and the intercarpal joints of the hands. The major semi-foundation joints include the articulations between the vertebrae and where the ribs articulate with the spine and sternum: the intervertebral, costovertebral, costosternal and costochondral joints.

The general characteristics of the foundation joints, and to a lesser extent the semi-foundation joints, are that they exhibit a small range of motion, are not under our conscious control, hold imbalances rather than resolve them, and cause the body to compensate around their imbalances.

Both the foundation and semi-foundation joints relate to tensions and forces in the body which may be either physical or vibratory in nature. To the extent that these joints deal with both structural and energetic forces, they are a major bridge between the bodies of energy and structure and, on a deeper level, between the wave and particle nature of these two bodies. These joints are of prime importance in any bodywork that deals with energy.

When these articulations become dysfunctional or are compromised, the body tends to compensate for the problem rather than resolve it. A restriction of motion of a foundation joint in the foot, for example, may cause stress or pain in the foot, and pain in the knee or hip. It may cause back pain, postural problems, or possibly some dysfunction elsewhere in the body. If the original restriction is silent, the cause of the other problems may not be apparent. Imbalances in one or more of the foundation or semi-foundation joints are very common and many of us unknowingly have compensatory limitations or problems from these joints.

Characteristics of energy and mind: tissue—held memory

When I went to osteopathic school in 1955, the "mind" was thought to be located in the brain; no one doubted it. Mind research focused on the dissection, electrical stimulation, and study of people with brain pathologies and anomalies. Memory was considered a function of the mind that was located in the brain. Since then many experiments, studies, and experiences, both within and without the medical community, have shown that mind and memory aren't nearly this simple, nor as easy to locate.

The body and the mind are inseparable. It no longer works to say that the mind is here and the body is there, nor to say that memory is here and the body is there. They are interlinked.

Systems of therapy that involve directly handling the body have revealed a portion of memory that is "body memory" or "tissue-held memory." The science of sports has highlighted the concept of "muscle memory." The memory aspect of the mind has a vibratory component that resides in the body tissue; it can be held locally or it may be held globally within the body. When you put your hands on someone, and are knowingly in touch with both their structure and vibration, you can literally work directly with both mind and memory through touch.

I personally discovered this in Rolfing where it is common for clients to recall long-forgotten events and circumstances when body tissues are stimulated. When there was a traumatic incident in an area, stimulation of that site often evoked a memory, sometimes a forgotten one. Tissue stimulation at some other location than the trauma might also activate that memory, suggesting that the traumatic imprint is a global phenomenon and not just local.

When I was eleven I sustained a double skull fracture when I ran into the side of a car on my bicycle. After recovery, I had post-traumatic amnesia with a lapse of memory extending from five minutes or so before the accident until I awoke in a hospital bed a number of hours later. I was unable to remember that period until thirty years later, when a portion of the memory returned during the seventh hour of Rolfing—the session devoted to the head. During that session I suddenly recalled incidents before and after the accident. I remembered getting on my bike and racing my friend down a long hill. I remembered waking up strapped on the operating table and bargaining with the doctors and nurses, if they would stop hurting me, I would lie still. These parts of my memory suddenly became clear, although I still could neither recall the accident itself nor the period immediately afterward.

Three years later I had an *unwinding* session given by a team of five of John Upledger's students, who were showing me the *unwinding* technique from his craniosacral systemtechnique. The session was entirely pleasant, in contrast to parts of the Rolfing session, which were very intense. Ten hands were placed on my body as directed by the team leader. My body began to move spontaneously and it seemed that I was gradually unwinding in slow motion like a coiled spring over a fifteen to twenty minute period. To my amazement, I regained full memory of the accident. I had hit the car broadside. I had an out-of-body experience before the ambulance arrived. I heard the conversations of the ambulance attendants during the ride to the hospital where I was x-rayed, taken to surgery and then wakened on the operating table.

With this *unwinding* session and the earlier Rolfing session my post-traumatic amnesia was gone and my memory was complete. It seemed that the memory freed itself from the tissues of my body where the traumatic vibration of the event had been imprinted. It had been released through the Rolfing session on my forehead and through the ten hands in the Upledger *unwinding* of my whole body. In the Rolfing I recalled the past experience during the actual Rolfing session itself. In the *unwinding* session I felt my body moving, but it was only after the session was over that the memories began to return. The two experiences were different but each felt right. In both I was just the observer.

Once I gave a Zero Balancing session to a 35-year-old woman with a six-year complaint of recurrent stiff neck and headache. The condition resulted from a sudden and unexpected manipulative move to her neck. Throughout the ZB session she allowed me to apply fulcrums and pressures to her body, which allowed me to go deeper and deeper into her structure and through her touch anxiety.

There came a point when I asked her to release fear and tension, and to recall as best she could the memory of the maladjustment six years before. I watched her body language closely. A deep breath signaled that she had completed her process. I then suggested she offer forgiveness to the practitioner who had been involved in the incident. I held the fulcrum in her neck throughout this period, giving her time to integrate the experience.

I saw her one year later. She reported that the headache and neck pain had not recurred since our session. My sense was that both the tissue tension and the tissue memory had resolved.

Thought as a Wave Form

I perceive thought as a wave form. In this model, thoughts, ideas, concepts, and belief systems are seen to have a vibratory component, and thereby have the ability to imprint in the fields of the body. To the extent we can get our fingers on these imprints, we can influence them. This leads to the possibility of interacting with a person on fundamental levels through touch, even as deep as their belief systems. The implications of this are profound.

If something is learned early in life, it is often accepted as being *the truth* and becomes the basis of a belief system. To fully grasp how this works, consider a child who early in life is taught by the parents that the world is a dangerous place. This is the parent's view, which, if the child takes as *the truth*, becomes an operative strategy for the child. The vibratory component imprints in tissue or in the field. It can be so concretized that it will remain held in configuration and affect a person's behavior both in general and in detail. It will become an operative program for that person.

An imprint can act as a focal point in the field, similar to a rock in a stream, and affect life, just as a fast-flowing current creates whirlpools and turbulence downstream. From the therapeutic point of view, if we can locate the imprint, we can bring a clear stronger field through it, and remove or alter its form. The person is then freer from that obstruction and behavioral changes can manifest.

Experience has shown that imprintsthrough touch and issues can be resolved directly through touch when clearer, stronger fields are brought through them. Change often happens on a subliminal level, where the content of the imprint never comes to consciousness. Energy work is certainly not a panacea for mental and emotional difficulty, but to the extent you can release held vibration, you can lessen the grip of an issue or problem and influence its resolution within the person. Vibrations shift; beliefs alter; behaviors change.

Imprints in the background field

Thoughts and emotions can imprint in tissue, or more generally in the background field. Consider the field of tension created in a family by the continuing discord between the parents. A child who is oversensitive to the volatility of the vibration might instinctively pull back from contact with this earth-plane reality. A portion of the child's energy literally withdraws from his feet and up his legs. The child's field contracts, resulting in weak energetic grounding, and less connection with the environment. Twenty or so years later, this person might come to a therapist and say, "I feel isolated, almost like I don't belong on the planet." The childhood strategy of pulling back from the earth has been carried into the adult as an ongoing experience of minimal, perhaps tenuous, connection to daily life.

In the Zero Balancing with Sara (related in Chapter 4), her request was to feel more powerful and less fearful. As a child she had been full of passion and energy, but early on got the message that her family couldn't deal with that behavior, and she dampened her natural exuberance. Evaluation showed she had decreased energy flow through her legs and into her feet.

Another child may have experienced sexual abuse, and as a survival strategy, pulled the vibration away from the pelvis or some specific area of the body. A vacuum might thus be created in the background field and the person may feel isolated from parts of her body.

A person who has been struck often, say around the head or the upper back, might implode the vibration, rather than withdraw from it, and cause an area of highly concentrated vibration in the field. These vibrations often hold emotions of anger, fear, hatred, and resentment.

These and other configurations can occur in the background field. They are met regularly in the therapeutic experience of body workers. Regardless of the exact cause or the specific configuration, releasing the vacuum, the compression, or somehow normalizing the field configuration, makes the person feel more complete, whole, and often more energized.

Working with Fields

Configurations in the energy body are created by circumstance and often our early, naïve, or even misinformed strategies for coping with the world around us. These configurations do not show on X-rays, MRI scans, or in any standard testing. Nonetheless they are real and can affect behavior or cause bodily symptoms. Energy can be blocked, deficient, or held in some particular configuration.

A man came to see me complaining of chest pain ever since he rolled his car in an accident five years ago. He had seen a number of physicians, had undergone X-rays, MRIs, and other tests. Everything was reported normal, yet the pain persisted. Palpation revealed the vibrational imprint of the seat belt across his chest. Over several visits, clearer stronger fields of energy were brought though the imprint. As it released, the pain resolved.

On another occasion I worked with a woman at the Esalen Institute in Big Sur, California. She was a physiotherapist, very amiable, about thirty years old. On the surface she seemed to be functioning well. She had a history of Crohn's disease, an inflammation of the small intestine. When she was twenty-one she experienced a traumatic period involving intestinal surgery. The trauma of that, and of subsequent surgeries, left a deep-seated anxiety, and a basic distrust and fear of touch. Her request from the session was to work with the issue of fear, in particular in reference to touch.

If she were in ongoing therapy, we would look at her earlier history that led to the Crohn's disease. But, for a single session, it did not seem appropriate to delve into history prior to the Crohn's disease. The immediate issue was that of touch, fear, and anxiety.

I began the Zero Balancing session. At my first touch, she became anxious and her body contracted. To honor her anxieties, and
to keep the subject of her uncertainty in the foreground of thought,
my strategy was to repeatedly ask permission to touch her. I felt
that each time she consciously gave me permission she would
lessen the grip of her past experiences. With permission I put my
fingers on her back and she began to tremble. I removed my hands,
the trembling stopped. I asked permission again to touch her. As I
did the shaking began again. I removed my hands and it stopped.
After a few repetitions of obtaining consent, touching her and coming off, the trembling response began to subside. Following more
repetitions something suddenly shifted, her body relaxed and the
touch began to feel good to her. I stepped back for a moment to let
her have that experience.

By the end of the session she was relaxed, enjoying touch, and
at times appeared to be in reverie. There were no signs of fear or
anxiety. When she came off the treatment table, she was glowing,
and seemed literally to be a different person.

Energy and Spirit: the Vitality of Vibration

Just as we can touch the mind and the emotions of a person, we can
also influence the spirit and vitality through touch.

Each person has an individual expression of vitality and spirit.
When the energy field is vibrant, coordinated, and focused, it leads
to behavior that reflects those qualities. When the field is vibrant
but discordant, the behavior might be frenetic and hyperactive.
When the field is flat, dull, and unfocused, it may express as a non-
specific depression. We can all picture how different fields of vibration might appear in reference to the behavior of friends and ac-
quaintances.

There are many ways to influence someone's spirit. In terms of
touch and the physical body, stimulation of bone is one of the most
effective ways. If a bone is stimulated, say by squeezing the ankle
bone in just the right way, the stimulus spreads throughout the
skeletal system. As a result, the person experiences more energy
globally in the body, perhaps as heat or tingling, and will feel more
alert, vibrant, and literally re-spirited.

We can work directly with the person's experience to influence spirit. For example, I worked with a woman in a workshop who had just pulled her back and was in a lot of pain. In addition to the back pain, she was depressed, lackluster, and dampened on the spirit level. She shared that her life was not working for her. Her past history was very sad and she seemed without hope or optimism. Her only child had died of leukemia ten years ago, and the month following her husband had died. Two years later she remarried and, though still in relationship, the marriage was non-supportive and unfulfilling. From her perspective everything she touched seemed to fall apart. Even on the first day of the workshop she had pulled her back and was now in a great deal of pain.

"I'm a failure," she said. "Everything I do fails. I never succeed."

Now, it turned out that she had quit smoking three days earlier. During the ZB, I commented, "You haven't smoked in three days. It sounds like there is some success in that."

"Is there?" she asked.

"Of course there is. You've had three days of success."

This was probably the first time in years that she had considered or heard the word "success" in reference to herself. Throughout the ZB I stayed with that theme. I moved slowly, and gradually amplified the experience of success.

"Feel the success of the last few days — and feel the sensation of my touch."

As I said that, I increased the pressure of my touch, being sure to involve bone. I held it steady and secure, being sure that it felt good to her. I wanted her to have the simultaneous body experience of the good feeling of my touch and her mental recognition of success. This provided a true here-and-now experience for her. To further amplify these effects, I removed my hands, and then encouraged her to take the feeling of success deep into her body. By the end of the session her back pain was much improved, and, in addition, everyone could see her becoming more vital and animated.

The next day she sat at the back of the class, free of pain, with a smile on her face and a sparkle in her eye. The amplified vibration and the success of not smoking had all begun to move through her. She left the workshop with a new sense of hope and optimism. She seemed re-spirited and turned in her life's direction.

Changing Energy and Changing Lives

If we conceptualize people in terms of particle and wave, and understand the functions of energy and the nature of its configurations, we see new ways of interacting with others or ourselves. A person whose energy is blocked or congested, or whose fields are chaotic or depressed, will have a harder journey through life than the person whose flows and fields are clear and organized.

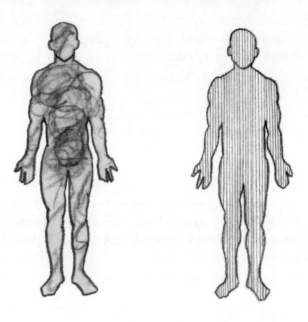

Energy fields vary in clarity

Therapies such as meditation, yoga, acupuncture, Zero Balancing, and other body handling systems can improve peoples' lives because they can literally change the configuration of energy and the clarity of its movement in the body. This line of thinking opens many doors into types of therapy and self-help activities. It strikes an optimistic tone in that we can be more proactive with our health and personal development.

Chapter Four

Zero Balancing Session with Sara

Fritz: Sara, are there any special issues that you would like to work with—on any level—body, mind, emotion, or spirit?

Sara: I'd like to look at being more powerful. I think I am powerful, but I don't claim it. Also I'm quite fearful and I would like to clear that.

Fritz: More power, no fear.

Sara: This feels like Christmas! *(laughs)* If you could do that, I think that would be great.

Fritz: I like it when someone refers to it feeling like Christmas. When I do a ZB I am often reminded of Christmas—you receive a beautiful package but you don't know the content until you open it. When you put your hands on a person, it is like opening a present; you don't know what's inside and are often surprised. ZB has the sense of discovery and adventure—like Christmas.

I would like to begin by asking you several questions? How old are you?

Sara: 32.

Fritz: Have you ever been married?

Sara: No.

Fritz: Are you in a relationship?

Sara: Yes.

Fritz: Good. Have you any brothers and sisters?

Sara: I have a younger brother.

Fritz: Are you good friends?

Sara: Hmm. *(pause)* Yes, we like each other. But we're very different, so we're not sort of friends.

Fritz: Was your childhood okay with him?

Sara: We used to have fights. But it was fun, we used to play together.

Fritz: As a general statement, would you say your childhood was easy or difficult?

Sara: I had times in my childhood that were very wonderful and magical, and there were frequent times when I was told to shut up. I had a lot of spirit that was dampened.

Fritz: Herein may lie a source of the feeling of a lack of personal power. This early conditioning of being dampened, to not be powerful, not to be in full bloom.

Sara: Exactly.

Fritz: I'll look for an energetic or physical representation of this particular disempowerment in the body, and if I find it I'll see if I can release it for you.

How is your physical health?

Sara: Great.

Fritz: Are there any health issues or other information that I should know about you before doing the ZB? Any problems, headaches or, body symptoms?

Sara: No. I have problems with my hips sometimes, they go a bit wobbly and out of sync.

Fritz: Do you have pain or lack of stability?

Sara: Hmm. I go to a chiropractor who works with the hip problem. It's pain, quite deep pain. And it happens on both sides.

Fritz: And how often do you need attention?

Sara: Once every six months or once every year.

Fritz (to everyone): With Sara's permission I would like to summarize where we are now. The basic frame of the session will be to look at personal power and issues of fear. We already have a few possible clues to the lack of power. I could continue to ask more personal history questions regarding the emotion of fear and search out where it's coming from. Or I could rely on palpating the body and exploring for a representation of fear under my fingertips.

As a ZB'er I want to find a palpable expression of the person's problem or request in the body — in this case, the lack of power or the issue of fear. I want to literally get the problem under my fingertips, so that I can use touch, create fulcrums, induce clearer fields of vibration, and thereby directly influence the problem. This is basic theory. What the outcome will be, time will tell.

I know that Sara has been receiving acupuncture and body work from Deirdre. Knowing the high quality of Deirdre's work I can assume that Sara has already cleared many things. As I work with Sara, it will not be with someone who has never had any touch or therapy, but with someone who has had a lot of very good therapy. Within that perspective I'll look to see if I can find a next step.

Fritz (to Sara): Let's begin. Please sit up on the table.

Standing behind Sara, Fritz evaluates the structural/energetic interface of the shoulder girdle by moving each of her arms in a circumduction motion. Finding this clear, he evaluates the pelvic girdle through side bending movements of the trunk, and finds a limitation of energy flow through the right sacroiliac joint.

Fritz (to everyone): This limitation is consistent with Sara's history of low back and hip discomfort, and may be the first place I have found that relates to her story.

At Fritz's request, Sara lies down, and he puts a pillow under her head, which meets with an approving smile.

Fritz: Your job is to just relax and enjoy the session. Take a few moments to yourself, and feel how good that feels.

Fritz picks up Sara's feet, and places a half moon vector through her body, then evaluates the movement of the ankles and the feet.

Fritz (to everyone): The half moon vector fulcrum reveals that there is a lack of energy flow down the lower legs, especially on the outside of the left leg. While this is not extreme, the decreased flow could give Sara the sensation of incomplete grounding and a certain lack of power. It could have come from a childhood strategy of dampening or dulling exuberance by pulling her energy away from the earth. Regardless of its cause, this energy configuration would be consistent with the feeling of not having full power.

To objectify his findings Fritz asks Deirdre to be his marker, and for her to repeat the half moon vector and make her own evaluation and conclusion. This she does and agrees to the lack of qi in the lower legs with the comment "thread, rather than elastic."

Fritz then asks Deirdre to rotate the ankles and feel the slightly restricted external rotation of both ankles, indicating Sara walks a bit on the outsides of her feet. Finally, he asks Deirdre to move both feet and feel for a slight locking in the bones. All of these findings are consistent with the decrease of qi in the lower legs and lack of full grounding.

Fritz (to everyone): None of us are symmetrical, and few people have total fluidity of body motion or energy flow. In evaluating the energetics of the body, we not only pay attention to the gross pathology and limitation of function or energy, but also to finer limitations and restrictions that would be considered within the normal range of physiology. With Sara, her gross functions are within medical norms. But from the energetic perspective the finer limitations may hold clues to held body imprints. These clues mark the starting point for our work today. At the end of the session we can evaluate for any changes which have occurred.

This is a lengthy way of saying to Sara that she is normal. We are talking about subtle limitations and restrictions.

Fritz goes on to evaluate the lower half of the trunk, from the lower rib cage down to the pelvis. He finds held tension around the right side of the 4th lumbar vertebra and the right sacroiliac joint and he offers several short (2-3 second) fulcrums. She smiles as he puts in the fulcrums.

Fritz checks the right leg rotation in the hip joint, and the energy of the right pelvic bowl. Internal and external rotation of the hip are good. In evaluating the pelvic bone, he finds held tension and puts a fulcrum in the pelvic bone itself.

Fritz (to Sara): This should feel good to you.

Sara: Hmm, great.

Fritz (to everyone, while repeating several short fulcrums): When a person holds tension in the bones of the pelvis, fulcrums there almost universally feel good. It is an area of the body which rarely gets touched. Most body systems fail to address held vibration within the pelvic bones. *Sara smiles contentedly.*

Fritz: Everything in ZB should either feel good, or hurt good. If it ever hurts bad, please tell me. I now have a fulcrum in the pelvis exactly on the acetabular ridge, releasing another area of bone-held vibration. From the perspective of ZB the fulcrum is a long fulcrum — ten seconds.

Sara: It feels really good.

Fritz (releasing the fulcrum): Let the feeling come into your body. Take the vibration back into yourself. It's yours. Feel your power increase as the vibration fills you.

Fritz steps back.

Fritz (to everyone): As you watch Sara, you can see her response to the release of vibration into her body. There are a number of things happening simultaneously. She is having a true, clear, pleasurable, multidimensional experience. She is feeling the pleasure of the fulcrums. She is taking vibration into her body and experiencing a sense of fullness. She is experiencing an increase of personal power.

Watch.

It's been over a minute and we haven't seen a closing signal yet — there is still very shallow breathing; she is still working. The fact that it is pleasurable means that she will be less inclined to block the event and that it will have a greater likelihood of permeating the whole person — the body, mind, emotions, and spirit. You can see her face flushing. The energy, the vibration, of the body is moving upward in her body as well as globally in her psyche. Even her inner child is being affected and becoming more empowered. The length of the working response indicates that this is a deep integration, and surely involves the level of the inner child. There is deep reorganization. *(Sara breaths in very deeply.)* There's the deep involuntary breath — our closing signal that the integration is complete.

Fritz (to Sara): How are you doing?

Sara: The sensation keeps getting stronger and stronger — like waves coming up. I feel very big. I feel like I'm huge.

Fritz (to everyone): Notice the increasing moisture in her eyes. I don't know exactly where it's coming from, but you can see from her demeanor that a few tears could be forming.

(Sara beams a big smile.)

Fritz: The feeling of bigness is the filling and expansion of the energy body from the release of the held vibration in the bone. The vibration fills the field. It expands, and Sara's literal experience is that she is bigger. Her energy body is expanding. It's expanding so much in fact that it almost squeezed tears from her eyes.

Fritz once again asks Sara how she is doing.

Sara: Okay. *The intonation is one of someone who has just processed a great deal.*

Fritz continues the session by moving over to her left side, to evaluate and balance the left hip and the left half of the pelvis.

Fritz: On external rotation of the left hip there is a small amount of tension held in the ligaments.

He puts a series of fulcrums into the left hip and pelvis. Then he again tractions the left leg to take up the slack from the body, and with his second hand places a fulcrum in the front of the pelvis on the left anterior superior iliac spine. Sara winces slightly, and Fritz carefully releases the tension in his touch to remain within the "'hurting good" parameter of Zero Balancing. He checks verbally with Sara to determine if the new pressure is okay, which she confirms. Fritz then completes the fulcrums in the hip and pelvis, quickening the pace as he does so, and moves down to the feet.

Before working with the feet themselves, he reevaluates the effect of the work done up to this moment with another half moon vector through the legs. He comments that there is about an 80 percent improvement of the energy and structure in the lower half of the body.

He then asks Deirdre to re-evaluate. She does so and comments with approval that Sara's legs feel much more even, and that they feel energetically fuller and bigger, all the way along, and that the uniformity goes throughout both legs to the pelvis.

Fritz: It feels like she's more in herself.

Deirdre: Absolutely.

He then asks Deirdre to check the ankles once more.

Deirdre: Wow.

Fritz: We know that even if we did nothing more, Sara's whole body is going to feel more supported, congruent, and stable. She is going to feel more powerful and be more effective in her life.

Fritz then goes down to the feet.

Fritz (to everyone): It's been my experience that many people hold childhood patterns in their feet; in particular within the intertarsal articulations. Earlier we noted a tendency to walk on the outer edge of the foot. I will now look for specific patterns which might represent her responses to being squashed as a child. If I find any, I will attempt to ascertain at what period of her life they occurred. I'll look for the earliest time in Sara's life when she began to concretize and hold those experiences in the feet. If I can find this, I'll put in a fulcrum, not only through the held patterns in the feet, but also through her experience of those events. I'll be working in several domains simultaneously — the here and now held pattern in the feet with its entrapped physical and psychological vibration, as well as with the unconscious mind and the experience of the past.

These patterns are usually held in both feet, typically more evident in one foot than in the other. I will release the superficial tension from both feet but will do the alchemical fulcrum only on the more involved foot.

Fritz evaluates both feet, and selects the left foot where he has isolated a clear pattern of childhood contraction.

Fritz (to everyone): To create the alchemical effect I will begin by putting a standard one-handed fulcrum into the intertarsal articulations of the foot, and engage the contraction. Holding that tension securely, I now slightly exaggerate the tension promoting more vibration, taking care to increase the strength of my hands to make a stronger container. Without losing my energy/structure interface, I now seek an event and/or a time under my hands. *(Pause)* Right there! I'm getting about four as the age. I'm locked into that moment. I now put a fulcrum through that event by adding a new direction of tension to the existing fulcrum I already have in place, without losing any of the vibration. In essence I am creating a new fulcrum in the area under my fingers. Now the pattern is releasing. I'm staying with it. The pattern is right now at its pinnacle. *(Sara's closed eyelids are moving rapidly at this point.)* There it goes. There is the release. I can now disengage from the fulcrums, in the reverse order of their creation.

Tom: What tells you that the age was four?

Fritz: Once you have an event isolated under your fingers you can mentally dowse back through time for the date or age. There are many ways to dowse. Holding the tension stable I count back in time until I get an internal signal that I was "there." I have a number of internal signals established for dowsing. The signal I used here was the sound of a "click" when I arrived at the age. Dowsing is not a specific Zero Balancing skill but I encourage people to learn the art. It can be a helpful tool.

Fritz (back to Sara): How are you doing?

Sara: I felt my heart beating strongly.

Fritz: There are a number of body signals in ZB which indicate the client is responding to the work. A faster or stronger heart beat is one of them. Regarding the event at age four you may or may not recall. If you do recall it, it verifies the experience and what we are saying. If you don't, it doesn't mean that nothing has happened. Years of experience has shown that it is common for releases and integration to take place on a subliminal level. The proof of success—the proof of the pudding—is not necessarily what you recall or remember but what happens to your behavior over the coming weeks or months. Pay attention and let us know. Only time will tell.

Fritz then integrates everything he's done thus far with a half moon vector through the legs, and moves up to the upper part of her body.

Fritz asks Sara how she is doing, paying attention to her voice vitality and listening for any indication of possible depletion of energy.

Sara (with a soft yet vibrant voice): I feel good.

Fritz continues the ZB with an evaluation half moon vector through her neck. He checks her upper back, and then assesses her neck movements. Following these basic evaluations, he returns to areas of tension in the upper back and neck, putting in short 2-3 second fulcrums as he goes. Sara continues to relax more deeply.

At one point he places a deep fulcrum in the top of each shoulder, in the area of the trapezius muscle, and suggests that she relax into the sensation, and let go of all responsibility. She grins and lets out a small giggle. There is a feeling of well-being throughout the whole room, which all experience. Sara has murmurs of contentment as the energy of "letting go" is experienced and acknowledged by all of us.

Fritz continues to hold the fulcrum in silence for some ten to twelve seconds. Sara's arms open and hang down from the table, but Fritz directs her to replace her arms on her chest, to contain her energy.

Fritz (to Sara): Do you feel the power under my hands? *Sara nods.* Experience the sensation that is there without adding to it.

Fritz (to everyone): The overlaying of the feeling of power from my hands, on a field of no personal action on Sara's part, draws on the principal and power of *non-action*. It will refill her power reserves, as it were.

He continues to work on Sara's head, neck, and upper back. Periodically Sara coughs when he has his hands under her ribs.

Fritz (to Sara): I'm just about done. How are you?

Sara: Fine.

Fritz: I plan to check your right hip again. Look over your body and see if there are any other places that still need attention.

Sara: My knees.

Fritz: Anything else?

Sara: My hands.

Fritz: Okay. Anything else?

Sara: My elbows.

Fritz: Anything else?

Sara: Toes. *(laughs)*

Fritz proceeds to check each of the above areas, putting in fulcrums where appropriate. He finishes the session by integrating with a half moon vector through the legs.

Fritz (to everyone): Because of the number of things which we have addressed in the session, and the depth to which we have gone, I want to amplify Sara's vibratory fields globally to help promote integration. I'll do this by squeezing firmly across both heel bones as I implement the half moon vector through her legs and body. This will give Sara a greater sense of containment, integration, and grounding.

Fritz releases his hold, and stands back from the table as Sara integrates the experiences. She begins to return to full consciousness and awareness.

Fritz: When you are ready, turn on your side and sit up slowly. Then in your own timing stand down and take a few steps. You are stepping onto a new planet.

Sara walks slowly and with the expression of someone who is walking for the first time.

Sara: I feel like I've got these huge muscles in my legs. (laughs)

Fritz: Walk across the room one more time, but this time walk as though you were walking into your future.

Sara walks like a mighty being. We all laugh.

Fritz: We have released and/or integrated a number of patterns during the last half hour. Your energy body is lined up through your physical body, and you are more fully integrated in energy and structure. Your feelings will probably reflect this. Look for increased confidence, more power, and more boldness. I would expect a noticeable change in your behavior.

Before finishing our time together, I'd like to ask whether any feelings of loss or grief came up for you in the latter part of the session. My curiosity was aroused by the few coughs you had when I put fulcrums in the rib area. Chest cough is often a sign of a grief issue.

Sara (about to say "no," pauses, then says): I had forgotten. I was young. My brother's friend had an owl, and he and my brother bought a little mouse to feed it on. *(pause)* They shot it . . . and I was really upset. I was friends with this mouse. I used to talk to it, and they killed it.

Fritz: Let me suggest in this moment that you let go of any grief around that event. As you let sorrow release from your system, forgive those surrounding you at that time for what happened. These thoughts came up to you during the session and are still available to influence. By releasing any sorrow, anger, or other emotions, and bringing forgiveness into the field, the held charges from the event can be reprogrammed in your memory bank.

Sara's report of the ZB experience

Fritz asked me what I would like to focus on during the ZB session and I said that I wanted to be more powerful and less fearful. As a child I had been full of passion and energy, but I'd got the message that my family couldn't deal with that, and I'd dampened my natural exuberance.

Fritz began by touching my feet and legs. He said that they felt "empty." As he touched me, I felt a slight sensation of warmth filling my legs and this intensified throughout the session and after it.

When Fritz moved up and held my pelvis on the right side, he talked to me and asked me to really take in the feeling of power. For the first time I actually went inside myself and concentrated on absorbing what I was feeling. It was as if waves of fire were sweeping up through my body and this got more and more intense, even though Fritz had stopped touching me. They were gold and red. I think Fritz mentioned myself as a child and I had an image of the little child inside me and what a wonderful relief it was for her to be given permission to be strong again. I could almost feel her leaping up in joy to greet what was coming in.

This all went on for quite a time and I was thankful to Fritz because he left me alone to take it in.

When he moved on I remember thinking, "Oh no! I'm going to experience even more power and I don't know what to do with it!" So when Fritz touched a point on my groin that was painful, I asked him not to apply so much pressure and that made me feel more stable and in control.

Then Fritz worked on my feet and said he was contacting an event in my childhood around the age of four. My heart began pulsing under his fingertips, but no memory came. On the other foot, Fritz said he had found something to do with my brother, but I wasn't conscious of what it might be.

After the session, Fritz asked me to get up and walk up and down. My legs felt those of a shot-putter! Very strong, solid, and huge. Inside my body was a golden and red light, but it wasn't floaty. It was strong, like flexible metal.

In fact, I didn't have any sensation of being diffuse or dreamy. I felt as though a black felt-tip pen had been drawn around the outline of my body. I was absolutely contained and sure of where I ended and where the outside world began.

Post Script July 2004

Sara: Looking back at this account after an interval of some years, I see the person I was then as very much still a child. It feels very far away from who I am today. I am now fully a woman — not fearless — but certainly strong, and I date that change as beginning with this ZB.

Chapter Five

Engaging Energy and Structure

The fundamental principle of Zero Balancing is that we are made up of particles and waves, which comprise our two bodies of structure and energy. Western scientific approaches to health and healing are mostly based on the structural aspect of our being. Eastern and some alternative approaches include the energetic aspect. Zero Balancing is related to both. I believe that if you are trained in structure, you need to recognize energy; if you are trained in energy, you need to recognize structure; if you know both, you can put them together.

Relating Structure and Energy

An easy way to put structure and energy together is to first distinguish them separately and then look at the relationships between them. Remembering that we use the word "tension" as a synonym for energy, imagine a rubber band in the palm of your hand, coiled and loose. You can see its structure, you can feel its structure, but there is no awareness of its energy or of any tension within the material. It is not until you pick up the rubber band and stretch it that you will feel its energy. As you stretch the material you may become aware that there are different stages of tension. In the first stage you just feel the tension. In the next stage you feel the active engagement of the band. Then you come to the stage where you are at the end of the stretch, beyond which the rubber band would break.

As kids we talked to each other through tin cans and string. Two tin cans, which had their tops removed and the bottoms in place, were connected together with a string attached to the bottom of each can. One of us would talk into a can while the second held his can to his ear. When the string was loose there was no sound transmission. When there was slight tension in the string a sound could be heard but it wasn't decipherable. But when there was enough tension in the string words became audible and clear communication was possible.

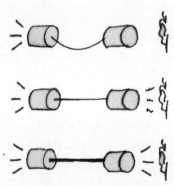

Tin can communication

In both examples it is clear that tension is needed to have the item perform its function. Tension is needed in a rubber band to have it hold things together, just as there had to be tension in the string to have sound waves transmitted. In Zero Balancing we have created the "blue line diagram" to represent these principles in terms of therapy and touch.

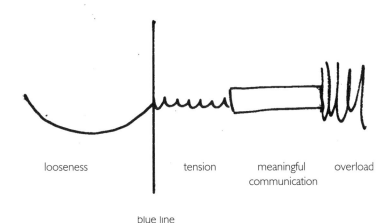

looseness   tension   meaningful   overload
communication

blue line

Blue line diagram

The blue line drawing summarizes the relationship of energy and structure in terms of touch. The curved line toward the left of the diagram represents being in relation to structure but not to energy. For example, assume an individual is relaxed and lying supine. This person remains passive as we pick up the arm. We would be aware of the structure of the arm, its weight, and the looseness or lack of tension if we moved it in one direction or another. As we continue to move the arm in any given direction we would come to a point where we engage the resistance of the trunk. This first encounter of tension or resistance is a very special place. It is our first awareness that we are in connection with something other than just the structural properties of the arm. It is the first touch with the energy of the other person, the first touch of another consciousness. We refer to this point as the "blue line."

Examples of the blue line are everywhere. It is a place we all know well. It is the first fragrance of dinner cooking; the first sound of your partner's voice after separation all day; the first sight of your child coming home from school. In a conversation it might be the *"aha"* moment when the true meaning or purpose of the communication first reveals itself. It might be the first nibble of a fish on the end of a fisherman's line.

Immediately to the right of the blue line in our illustration is an area where we have engaged both the energy and the structure. The amount of tension here is ideal to evaluate the relationship of energy to structure, but not enough to make significant change in that relationship. In terms of the body there is enough tension here to get insight into the function of a part without having a deep enough connection to promote major change.

Further to the right represents the relationship of energy to structure needed to effect meaningful change, represented by the "box." The amount of tension needed for change is not just one exact point or amount, but is represented by an area of degrees of tension, which allows for variation and individuality of touch. Touch within this area, within the box, must meet several criteria. First, it must engage both the body of energy and the body of structure in a meaningful way. Second, it must have clear boundaries so that both energy and structure can be individually identified. Third, it must feel good to both the receiver and giver, acknowledging that touch toward the extreme right of the box may "hurt good" to the receiver.

The extreme right of the diagram, the area outside the box, represents overload. The pressure here is too strong, too deep, or too intense. In this area the client will consciously or unconsciously draw away from us, away from our touch. The effectiveness of the session will drop. As long as touch is in the box, even where it "hurts good," the person will be open to our efforts. But unpleasantly painful touch encourages resistance and reaction.

Everyone has a touch preference, both the giver and receiver. I personally like to be touched deeply and tend to touch others that way. You may prefer to receive and give a lighter touch. There is no value judgment about which is better as long as the touch meets the criteria for being in the box. Early in a session you need to establish the depth of touch that is satisfactory to the client and to yourself.

Fulcrums

The fulcrum is a working tool of touch. Specifically it is a field of tension that we create through touch by lifting, pulling, pushing, twisting, bending, sliding, or compressing structure. Tension in Zero Balancing refers to the pressure of opposing forces. Any manner of creating tension can be used as long as it meaningfully involves both the bodies of energy and structure. The theory is that we maintain clear boundaries with the opposing forces that we have engaged, thereby creating a relationship with them. We work with the client's own energy within his or her body. We do not attempt to add energy into their system, nor take it away. In this sense a fulcrum is analogous to a catalyst in that it stimulates change but is not permanently affected by it.

Classifications of fulcrums

There are three (sometimes overlapping) classes of fulcrums: those which work as a point of reference to promote balance and change; those which act as a field to effect change; and those which act as a moving tension to work with the client's own energy to promote change.

A fulcrum as a point of reference

The simplest of the fulcrums are simple lifting fulcrums that act as a point of reference and a balance point. There are three dictionary definitions that give insight into this type of fulcrum. The *American College Dictionary* defines a fulcrum as "the support, or point of rest, on which a lever turns." The *American Heritage Dictionary* expands the concept of a point to "an agency through or around or by means of which vital powers are exercised." The *Oxford English Dictionary* broadens the idea further by saying a fulcrum is "a means by which influence is brought to bear."

A fulcrum as a point of reference

With your partner supine, slide your open hand, face up, under your partner, and locate a rib. Raise one finger up onto the rib with enough pressure to be securely yet comfortably felt by your partner. Hold this stationary for several seconds, and then release. You have just created a fulcrum.

On the structural level, as the fulcrum is held stationary, it acts as a balance point, like the support of a see-saw, with structure being allowed to move in reference to that point. Local change occurs in and around the fulcrum. Change also occurs elsewhere in the body. In all interrelated systems one change sets others in motion, or gives an opportunity for this to happen. In medicine there is an axiom that when one joint is in trouble the joints immediately above and below it share some of the problems; there is a compensatory relationship. In family systems, when one family member is in trouble, other family members are affected in one way or another. In all interrelated systems, it comes down to this: when change occurs in one part of the system, it opens the possibility for other changes to occur.

On the energetic level, if the bone is holding excess vibration, the fulcrum will release some of the excess. The tension at the tip of the finger, which is in contact with bone, promotes release of the client's held vibration. This dispersed energy will go back into the general energy pool of the client. At times the client will have an experience of this release of energy. In the ZB session with Sara, for example, excess vibration was held within her pelvic bone. When this vibration was released back into her field, she not only displayed a number of objective working signs, but also described her subjective experience of feeling the waves coming up in the body, and causing her to feel very big—actually huge.

On the psychological level, these vortices of vibration often contain tissue-held memories. As the tension is released so is its held emotional content. These old impressions may or may not come to consciousness. When Ida Rolf worked on the area of my old facial trauma, I had recall of earlier events. Similarly, Sara recalled the incident of a mouse being killed and fed to an owl. In many cases, however, there is no memory recall. A memory may be insignificant, or, on the other extreme, imprinted so deeply that on release they do not come to conscious awareness.

In my years of practice I have had the opportunity to follow the progress of a great number of people over long periods of time. In doing so I found that, as a group, ZB clients became more psychologically stable and generally less stressed in challenging times. My assumption was—and is—that repeated sessions had released tissue-held memory, and that their fields were clearer and more organized. This was reflected as greater calm and generally more harmonious behavior. I remember once referring to Zero Balancing as a "subliminal system" because so much clearing seemed to occur without ever coming to conscious recognition.

A fulcrum as a field

The second general class of fulcrums refers to those that create a field of tension and thereby affect broad areas of the client's body. The most common way to create a field is with a straight pull, a curved pull, a compressive motion, or combinations thereof.

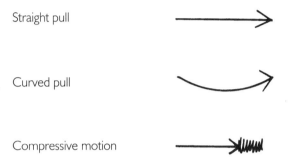

Straight pull

Curved pull

Compressive motion

In body work a curved pull is of particular importance in that it has a special relationship to both structure and energy. On the level of body structure, a curved pull relates to the curves in the body, such as the normal curves of the spine. On the level of energy, the curved pull relates directly to energy in that the natural movement of energy is in the form of a curve. Energy moves as a wave, as is evidenced in light, sound, or the waves in the ocean. Given that one component of a wave is a curve, a curved form has a natural relationship to energy. The curved pull is so important in Zero Balancing that it has been designated a special name, a "half moon fulcrum" or a "half moon vector," based on the curved image of a half full moon.

Half moon vector

The technique to create a half moon vector is to apply a tension in a curved direction rather than in a straight line. The actual experience of doing this makes the concept clear. Simply reach in front of you with both hands and pretend that you are pulling something towards yourself. First pull it in a straight line. Then pretend you are pulling in a curved line. Repeat this several times and it soon becomes apparent the kinesthetic difference between the two moves.

Pull towards yourself with a straight pull   Pull towards yourself with a curved pull

With a partner lying supine, stand at the foot of the table. Position your hands in the natural hollow just above his heel bones and pick up the legs and feet. Raise the legs to the height of an inch or two off the table and apply just enough traction with a <u>straight pull</u> to where you first meet solid resistance of structure. Stop. Up to this point you are just getting into position to create the half moon fulcrum. You have taken the looseness from the body and are at the blue line. Now, without loosing any of the tensions you have created, pull further towards yourself with a <u>curved pull</u>. Use enough tension to feel solidly connected with the person. Stop. The fulcrum is now in place. Hold all tensions for 3–5 seconds and then gradually release, set the legs back on the table, remove your hands, and rest. You have just created a half moon fulcrum.

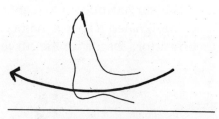

Curved pull to create a half moon vector

To further clarify the kinesthetic experience of what a half moon vector feels like, give yourself a contrasting experience. Keep all of the variables the same, excepting the form of the final pull. Specifically, pick up the legs and, with a gentle, straight pull, take the looseness out of the structure, progressing as described to the blue line. Stop. The experience now changes. Pull towards yourself with a straight traction, rather than a curved one. Pull with the same amount of tension as before and hold it for an equal period of time. Then release the tension and lower the legs back down on the table. Compare the two experiences.

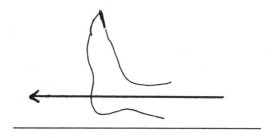

Straight pull, for comparison to the curved pull

Typically the two pulls provide very different experiences for both the practitioner and the client. For most practitioners the straight pull seems harder to accomplish. It actually requires more muscle effort in the arms, shoulders, and scapulae. It is not as comfortable, does not seem to engage the whole person, and does not feel as intuitively correct. For the person on the table the straight pull often feels more mechanical, less relaxing and engaging, and frequently seems to stop at the knees or hips rather than involving the whole body. It is generally less satisfying for both parties. Try it for yourself, both as a giver and receiver.

The curved form of the vector not only relates to the normal curves of body structure and to the natural movement of energy, but it also integrates the two bodies of energy and structure with one another. Thus the principle of a curve is used over and over in the form of the half moon vector.

In Zero Balancing this fulcrum is used in many ways and places. It is applied through the legs near the beginning of a session to engage the client fully. It gives the client a feeling of inner connectedness and wholeness, as well as a sense of a clear connection with the practitioner. A similar half moon vector is used halfway though the session to integrate energy and structure, and all the changes that have been made up to that point. It is used again in the closing sequence to integrate the whole session and to anchor it more deeply into experience. In addition, a half moon vector is used to work with the neck and upper back, to balance the bones of the hands and feet, and to address broad areas of the body.

When a half moon vector is held stationary, the tension within the curved field will organize fields in the client's body. Remember how metal filing particles react to a magnet passed beneath them. Things line up along lines of tension. In the body, both the physical particles and energy waves become more coherent and organized as they encounter the fields of the half moon vector.

Fields orient to lines of tension

A fulcrum as a moving tension

A third and last type of fulcrum is the moving fulcrum. In this fulcrum we engage the client's own energy as our working tool. As described in a moment, we gather their energy into a bolus and then move this through their tissue. A moving fulcrum can be created almost anywhere in the body but is most typically used to address soft tissue rather than bone. The effects of the fulcrum are to open, release and/or organize the client's held tension.

A moving fulcrum

You can demonstrate a moving fulcrum on yourself. The idea is to create a bolus of tension (energy) and then move it through your tissue. Reach down the outside of your lower leg where it is easy to contact muscle tissue. Curve your middle (your strongest) finger and contact the muscle tissue with the ball of your finger. Press firmly into the leg muscle so you have a good connection, and begin to move your finger up towards the knee. As you begin to move with firm pressure, feel tension gather in front of your finger. This is a bolus of energy. Continue to move it up the leg, in front of your finger, through the muscle tissue, until you get to the bone of the knee. Release your pressure and come off.

In an exercise such as this it may be difficult to separate what you are feeling with your finger and what you are feeling in the leg. It is often clearer to do this with someone else, where you can separate out what you are feeling from what is felt. Work with a partner and both perform and receive this exercise.

You can also demonstrate what a moving, fulcrum is in terms of your neck. With your right hand reach behind your neck and contact the left side of your neck with three fingers. The place of contact is on the lateral most aspect of the neck, just anterior, or in front of, the muscle tissue. Make a deep, firm, yet comfortable, connection with the neck tissue and begin to move your fingers towards the midline of the back of the neck. Within the first half or one inch create tension in front of your fingers, and move the tension in front of your fingers through the tissue back to the midline and then release the tension.

The skill needed for a moving fulcrum is the development of a bolus of energy and then moving it through tissue. Early on I referred to the fact that when I received a Rolfing from Ida Rolf herself she did not hurt as others did. My conjecture is that in front of her finger or elbow she had engaged my energy body, and that this vanguard of vibration opened my fields so that when her structure arrived a microsecond later there was an experience of pressure but not of pain.

Evaluation

Evaluation of a body part is important in bodywork when working with energy and structure. It indicates where fulcrums are needed and gives immediate feedback as to their effectiveness. As we shall see, evaluation and reevaluation remove guesswork and actually guide the number and types of fulcrums.

The depth of touch is different for evaluation than it is for a fulcrum. In referring to the blue line drawing, the depth of touch for evaluation is located between the blue line and the box; the tension of a fulcrum is greater as indicated by being in the box. In truth, the actual difference of pressure between evaluating and balancing may at times be small, but there is a fundamental difference between the actions. There is a huge mental shift between these two activities. In evaluation, the therapist pays attention to the incoming information perceived through palpation. The mind is in a receiving mode. In balancing, the therapist makes an action. The mind set changes 180 degrees from receiving to doing.

The receiver is often aware of the difference. During evaluation, the touch may seem superficial, non-defined, rapid, and perhaps even impersonal or vague. When the therapist shifts mindset and places a fulcrum, the experience of the client is one of security, engagement, and purpose. As the fulcrum is held in place it may simply feel good or it may evoke deeper responses such as emotion, forgotten memories, or an expanded state of consciousness.

Signature

When evaluating energy within tissue it is helpful to know the signature of energy. A signature is an identifying characteristic or characteristics. For example, in terms of a rose, odor is a signature. A rose smells like a rose. It is a dependable identifier. A consistent recognizable proprioceptive finding on palpation can be considered a signature. In learning signatures, educate your fingers, not just your mind, to identify proprioceptive signals, and learn to respond directly to the "feel of things."

For example, bone can hold localized areas of excess vibration. To the palpating finger, this vortex of excess vibration feels denser than the surrounding bone tissue. Sometimes it even feels like a small mass or elevation on the bone; other times it may feel like a small pea or tiny piece of gravel. Regardless of the words we use to describe the palpatory sensation, it has a specific feeling in terms of touch. Once you have identified this for yourself, it will feel the same to you everywhere you find it. The quantity or intensity of vibration may vary, but the quality of its feeling — the signature — the sensation to your palpating finger — will be the same.

Bone can have a localized area of deficient vibration, which has a signature to touch. I am not speaking here of situations like osteoporosis or bone lesions which are identifiable on x-ray or other tests, but about more subtle findings of local vibratory deficiency. This is not as common as excess vibration but it is not rare. The touch signature in bone of deficient vibration is a sense of dullness and lack of vitality or resilience of the tissue. There may even seem to be an indentation in the bone or the bone may have a fragile or insubstantial feel.

Energy in ligaments has proprioceptive signatures. An example of this can be seen in terms of evaluating the end ranges of motion of a joint. Move a joint to where the ligaments first engage, up to the blue line, and stop. Then move the joint slightly further in the same direction, heeding the feel of the tension in the engaged ligaments. It takes only a little practice to ascertain whether the ligaments feel too loose, too tight, or just right—or to say this in another way, to ascertain whether there is too little energy, too much energy or the correct amount of energy in the ligaments. These are the signatures of ligament tension. If this were the baseline evaluation, after placing one or more fulcrums, you could reevaluate the ligament tension and have immediate feedback of the effectiveness of the fulcrum and whether more work is needed or not.

Working with Fulcrums

Evaluation indicates where to place fulcrums. If an area of bone is holding a locus of excess vibration, the direct pressure of a lifting fulcrum will cause the excess vibration to lessen or release. On a rib, for example, I identify the area of excess, remembering that it has a distinct signature to touch. I lift up into it with the tip of my finger, holding the pressure for several seconds, and then release. The signals of a successful fulcrum are that on reevaluation the feel of the excess vibration will have changed, and the area will be less tender to the client.

If the bone has a locus of deficiency vibration, there is a variation of the fulcrum. The principal of this in-filling fulcrum is to create an energy vacuum under the finger into which energy will flow. Specifically, I identify the deficiency in a rib, and lift up into the area with my fingertip as though doing a standard lifting holding fulcrum. I make a secure contact with the energy and structure of the bone. I then make a micro-movement downward to slightly lessen the pressure on the bone while maintaining enough pressure to keep a solid bone contact. This creates an energy vacuum under my finger even though the fulcrum is still in place. I hold stationary for several seconds and then come off. Vibration will move into the deficiency.

A person often exhibits significant working signs of apnea/ hyperpnea and or rapid eyelid flutter during or after the fulcrum. With hands off the body, I give the person a moment to complete these signs before moving on. There are times that the in-filling can be felt as it occurs. At other times, perhaps more common, nothing special is felt during the fulcrum. But, almost invariably, when the area is reevaluated a few moments later, it feels fuller, denser, and more vibrant. When the area is checked on a subsequent visit weeks later the deficiency will be lessened, and perhaps even gone.

Building a Fulcrum

Fulcrums which are created with simple lifting or pressing forces only engage one dimension of the area being touched. If we want to engage a part more fully we can build a fulcrum. The theory in building a fulcrum is to superimpose one field of energy on top of another, and thereby create a field that has enough dimensions or tangents of energy in it to relate to those of the structure engaged.

The principles of this type of fulcrum can be illustrated in regards to the hip. In a typical session I want my fulcrum to engage the hip joint in three dimensions, front to back, top to bottom, and side to side. I begin by putting straight traction on the leg and thereby into the supporting ligaments of the hip joint. Hold this tension. This influences the molecules and vibration to line up along the force lines created by the pull. I hold this in place and then rotate the leg to induce a rotary force into the ligaments around the hip joint, which superimposes one field on top of another and engages the hip in all planes. These combined forces represent the fulcrum, which I hold stationary for a few seconds. The structural components and the vibratory fields of the hip, which are less strong than the forces applied through the fulcrum, will tend to align and orient to the organized field of the fulcrum.

A Fulcrum as a Working Force

A fulcrum becomes a working force when it is held stationary. It is during this stationary period that the forces of the fulcrum influence the client's body; it is here that alignment and change begins to occur. The principle of holding a fulcrum stationary applies in a straightforward manner to the first two classes of fulcrums, those lifting fulcrums that act as points of reference and those that work with fields. In terms of the third class, the moving fulcrums, the stationary period is represented by the constant speed or constant pressure that you maintain with the fulcrum.

How long do you hold a fulcrum stationary? Energy tends to move rapidly and as a result most of the fulcrums need only be held stationary for short periods. In Zero Balancing we think in terms of seconds and not minutes. An average fulcrum is held for one, two or three seconds. Some fulcrums may be held as long as ten seconds and, under very special circumstances, perhaps for as long as thirty seconds.

Repeated short fulcrums are more effective than a few longer or deeper ones. Each fulcrum tends to make a local change, which sets other changes in motion. Once things are set in motion in this way, a general movement of change is carried throughout the body, independent of any one particular fulcrum. Repeated short fulcrums enhance these movements, like short pushes on a ball that keep it moving.

If you hold a fulcrum too long it may cause your hands or body to hurt or become fatigued. This is especially true in working with larger or heavier people. If you ever experience fatigue or discomfort, release the tension you are holding. You should never sacrifice your body for someone else when doing therapy. If you are distracted by your own body signals, it becomes very difficult to hold or stabilize a fulcrum. Your effectiveness drops off, despite attempts to make it work. Moreover, if you disengage gently from a fulcrum while it is still working, its effect usually continues as though you were still in contact.

Do not gauge how long to hold a fulcrum by waiting for a working body signal to occur. You do not hold a fulcrum waiting for something to happen. As a general statement the main gauge in determining how long to hold a fulcrum is length of time. The client response is a reflection of a fulcrum or series of fulcrums, which may not actually occur during the fulcrum itself.

Exiting

Whenever you disengage from a client, make sure you have a clear, clean disconnection. This applies whenever you disengage your touch, be it from evaluating a part, completing a fulcrum, or when finishing a full session. Some body systems actually want to keep an energetic connection through the whole session. Massage is a good example where the masseur may want to maintain body contact for the full session. In Zero Balancing the situation is different. You work from interface where clear boundaries are the rule, and fully disconnect from each touch contact. Your general attention to the client and to the session maintains your engagement so that the client never feels deserted as you remove your touch.

At the end of a session pay particular attention to your final disconnection. It helps here to exaggerate your final bone connection with the foot and then consciously disconnect from that. With an extra clear bone connection, it is easier to make a clear disconnection. The hands-on portion of the session is then complete and the touch boundaries are clear.

Closing

The skill of relating energy to structure in evaluation and in creating fulcrums offers a remarkable range of possibilities for working effectively with body, mind, and spirit. I wish we were in a classroom together and had the opportunity to work out these energy principles through hands-on demonstration and instruction. It requires many words to describe something that can be felt or accomplished in a few seconds. Fulcrums can affect the structure itself, the energy itself, and the relationships between the two. They can release local and compensatory problems and patterns in the body. They can have psychological and behavioral implications as they release imprints of trauma, memory, and childhood conditioning. They can set long-term change in motion, and even be used to future pace a person in their activities. But in all of this, keep in mind that you are a catalyst. You set the stage; the client does the work. Your job is to create an opportunity, a focus, and balance around which a person can respond and change in harmony with their own system.

Chapter Six

Zero Balancing Session with Tom

Fritz: Hello, Tom. I look forward to doing a Zero Balancing session with you this morning. Having watched some of the other ZBs you have an idea as to the breadth of the work. Is there anything in particular you would like to work on, address, or process? How can the session best serve you?

Tom: I'm in a strange state at the moment. I feel very expanded. Quite shivery. Excited. Open. Aware. The whole house is vibrating. I've been thinking about this in preparation for this session and what I thought was — that I'd like that if you could . . . *(laughs)* . . . I know you can . . . *There is group laughter.*

I'd like you to put something of your touch into my practice of reflexology. Anything in that direction would be really very nice.

Fritz: Fine. *(pause)* About what you are feeling at the moment — this feeling of being open and expanded — is this just at this moment or has it been for the last hour, or day, or week, or longer?

Tom: It's from this occasion of all of us working together. I associate my openness and excitement with both our working in such a "pure" fashion, and from watching—from participating in—the ZB sessions you do. There is such an accumulation of sensations.

Fritz moves to place his hands on Tom's back for a moment and then disconnects and continues to speak.

Fritz: I don't quite know what the words are. The fact that you are already expanded, open, and electric means you are in an impressionable, vulnerable place. My issue is to provide your body impressions through my hands that will truly serve both your outer reflexology practice and your inner Buddhist practice. At the moment, I'm not quite sure what those feelings are but certainly they include feelings of self-worth, feelings of being part of a bigger picture, knowing that you're connected with something beyond yourself, and knowing that you are part of the whole. Of course you know all this already but giving your body the experience of being connected, while you're expanded, will anchor you deeper into your self-knowing.

Fritz returns to connect with Tom and pauses, keeping his hand in contact with Tom's left shoulder.

These are the thoughts that are going through my mind as I begin the session.

Fritz (to everyone): Part of the session will focus on Tom's impressions of my touch and how those impressions can directly affect his reflexology work. I would like my touch to feel so good to Tom that he will appreciate his body—himself—even more than before and thus gain an experiential understanding of how he can give this experience to his clients.

Fritz completes the side bending evaluation, and Tom lies down. Fritz does a half moon vector through the legs and goes on to evaluate Tom's lower back and pelvis. He checks the abdominal area and then begins to focus on the front right side of Tom's pelvis.

Fritz (to everyone): I want to direct part of this Zero Balancing towards the inner child. To let the inner child sense some of the knowing the adult Tom has come to know.

As Fritz continues to work, Tom's mouth opens slightly and his face has an expanded and open expression.

Fritz (to Tom, patting Tom's leg reassuringly): Your job is to just enjoy yourself. When my touch feels particularly good, let those feelings work into your body.

Color floods into Tom's face. Fritz continues into the session. He evaluates and applies fulcrums into Tom's right hip joint and leg, and then the left hip joint and leg. He then contacts Tom's outer left thigh with his middle finger and slowly moves energy down the outside of the leg, along the gallbladder meridian. Tom's head lolls to the side and a look of deep contentment crosses his face. Fritz pauses and just holds Tom's leg.

Fritz: Feel the real deep sense of peace that is occurring and the deep sense of trust that it evokes.

Fritz then goes to Tom's left foot and moves the foot in a myriad of ways — ways that are not typical of most ZB sessions: twisting, bending, probing, holding, stroking, and rubbing. He works with the soft part of his fingers, then the tips of his fingers. Thumbs probe and rotate into Tom's foot. It seems that every possible angle is covered.

Fritz (to Tom): This is to give you the experience of your own foot — your movement potential and some sensation potential.

Tom looks like he is experiencing a delicious array of sensations.

Fritz puts a single fulcrum into the left foot, then moves to the right foot. There he repeats a myriad of movements, massages the foot, and finally puts in a deep two-handed fulcrum. Tom looks serene as if he's fallen away somewhere in heaven. He releases a long breath and his head moves to the center of the pillow, aligning itself with the rest of his body.

Fritz: Realize how much you offer your friends and clients as you work with reflexology.

Fritz then performs an integrating half moon fulcrum through the legs and moves to the top of the table.

Fritz: How are you doing?

Tom: Hmm, fine.

Fritz begins to work under Tom's upper back and shoulder blades.

Fritz: Let go of any nervous tension, especially around your feelings of responsibilities at work. Let those tensions go.

Fritz places a moving fulcrum along the occipital ridge and works into Tom's occiput and neck. At one point he presses down on Tom's shoulders and a rush of emotion rises, turning Tom's face momentarily red. His mouth opens wider and he looks calm and peaceful. Fritz does the special head-heart fulcrum — grasping the suboccipital ridge with one hand

and contacting the body of the sternum with the other. He then slowly creates a half moon tension between his two hands, holding it for a number of seconds. Fritz then releases the contacts and sits back in the chair waiting. Tom looks very far away.

Fritz goes back to working under the thorax, and the soft tissues of the upper chest around the pectoralis major and minor muscles. He again works into Tom's neck and, as Fritz places Tom's head down, there is a sudden change in Tom's expression. A look of great dignity comes over his face.

Fritz then begins to massage his ears. There is a long suspension of movement and then Tom lets out a deep breath. He looks very, very peaceful.

Fritz: Good. Let the magnificence of life fill you. *(long pause)* Maybe even let it overwhelm you a bit. *A smile appears on Tom's face. A gentle gasp and a quiet internal flow of bubbling laughter and joy releases. His arms drop out over the couch. He stays still for a short while, enjoying his internal process.*

After a little time, Fritz begins to put his fingers to work once again under Tom's thoracic cage. Tom raises his hands back on his rib cage, as his eyelids flicker indicating significant internal activity. Fritz continues to place repeated brief fulcrums into the ribs and Tom's eyelid flicker begins to deepen. Something is clearly getting ready to release.

Fritz returns to work under the shoulders. Suddenly, like a man who has found what he was looking for, he places a deep fulcrum into both scapulae.

Fritz (to Tom): Drop into my hands and let me have the adult responsibility which you prematurely took on in childhood. Just let me have it. *A flood of emotion shakes Tom's body.* Just let me have it. As a man, that premature responsibility doesn't serve you any longer.

Slowly, ever so slowly, Fritz continues to raise and expand his hands under the scapulae. Then he begins to very gradually withdraw his hands from under Tom's back, puts his hands down, and closes his eyes for a few moments.

Tom sighs with relief, his eyes moisten and a tear moves gradually down his face. This single teardrop belies the extent of the release that can be felt tangibly in the room. A peaceful, relaxed expression comes over Tom's face and the room is very silent. Fritz opens his eyes and gently strokes Tom's right shoulder.

Fritz: Time to close.

Fritz closes the session according to protocol and ends with a half moon fulcrum through the legs. Slowly Tom sits up.

A softly spoken "Wow" escapes from his lips, followed by "Thank you" and then "Jesus! Fritz." They smile warmly at each other. Slowly Tom gets to his feet and begins to walk up and down beside the table.

Fritz: Let the inner child come up.

At that precise moment, a cat lets out a high pitched squeal and we all laugh. Nature reflects the profound dynamic of the session with a spontaneous synchronicity.

Another good morning's work reverberates outward into the universe.

Tom's report of the ZB session

Part of the session was a lesson in touch. Part of the session was a search. A search, while I was experiencing it, for ways of describing the session: the writer's habit, accentuated because I knew I would do what I am doing now, trying to describe it, searching for words where there are no words. Looking back, moments and sensations recur in no particular sequence. The garden chimes chording once, both clearly and faintly. The feeling of a tear running infinitely slowly down the side of my face. Fritz's voice, with compassion and understanding, saying, "Oh ... oh ... oh," as I fell through a hole in the world and was caught in his hands.

The hands are so strong: so big, quick, assured, competent, certain. The touch is completely precise and completely compassionate. It doesn't look for where to go. It goes. It is already there. The fulcrums are like music, except that music is time-bound and sequential. The hands move on the body and there is the feeling of a gorgeous cat stretch; they move again, minimally, and the cat stretch acquires a harmonic, a chime within the chime; they move again, a twist in time, and you fall through a hole in the world.

So maybe it's more like sculpture, not time-bound, but tactile, and made by hands. But the body-mind is so much more plastic and multi-dimensional. You can only experience sculpture from the outside. You experience this from the inside. You're inside it. It is you.

Part of it was gaps in consciousness. No, in the fabric of experience. Tears come, and it thinks: "Ah, look, tears." Fritz said,

"Let the magnificence of life fill you. Maybe even let it overwhelm you a little." My whole sensory system turned into one enormous gulp of joy. At this point, I remember, the observing mind checked out in pure shock and didn't return for the duration.

At another point, fairly early on, the image arose of a drawing I happened to look at yesterday: it's Eric Gill illustrating the lines from Donne, *"I am a little world made cunningly / Of elements and an Angelic spirit."* The rational mind, you see, under serious threat, grasps at literature to save it. The drawing is a small naked being whirling in the maelstrom of creation with huge creating hands conducting the entire scenario. I was deeply moved by this perfect image of the subjective sensation of being inside that body (that spaceship) at that time under those hands. After that, things got more intense and went somewhat beyond literature. As I said, the rational mind checked out.

At the end, when Fritz asked me to . . . something about dropping responsibility? Just when I thought it was all over? Well, that isn't there in my mind. I can't even remember what he said. I think I remember falling through the table, while all the time being held. What there is, what remains, is a nice space where it isn't. In the same way that you can't remember pain, once it has gone: there is just a comfortable space where it is not.

And, as I said, a lesson in touch; a lesson that can only be conveyed in touch.

So I will finish by saying this: it really is true. It really does work.

Chapter Seven

Memory Held in the Body

Memory can be held directly in the body. I believe that a portion of our memory and information is stored in our body as vibrational imprints in our tissues and in our fields. In one sense our body is like litmus paper and life imprints on us. Many of these imprints and impressions are registered through the medium of vibration and, as we will see, may be held in a variety of ways. But unlike the passivity of litmus paper, we have the ability to enhance, reduce, alter, or remove the vibratory imprints and impressions, and change their effect on our behavior and function. We are learning that part of the human condition includes our ability to reconfigure these fields and thereby change our internal attitudes and external behavior. We can become more responsible for our own human condition.

Memory, emotion, and experience imprint on the energy fields of the body. Although a myriad of vibrations just wash through the body causing a momentary ripple before moving on, without lasting consequence, many do imprint. This can happen in a number of ways, in any tissue, organ, or non-specifically in the background field. These imprints can keep a memory, emotion, or event anchored and alive in the person's behavior and psyche.

The location of tissue memory is based partially on how we received the original information. If we accept something as truth, it moves into our body without hindrance. It can go deep. When we resist something, it tends to lodge in the tissue that resists it.

Soft tissues of the body (the muscles, ligaments, and the body organs) are reactive tissues. When vibration impinges on them they can expand, contract, or in some way interact with the vibration. In theory, information that enters the field and imprints on a reactive tissue or organ will be held closer to consciousness than with a non-reactive tissue. Bone and periosteum, and to a lesser extent cartilage, are non-reactive tissues. They do not have the ability to contract, shut down, or block vibration. All they can do is receive imprints, which bury deeply.

Bone

Issues of self-identity, deep feelings of purpose, and our sense of personal security are located in our bones. The skeleton allows us to stand upright in the world, so issues concerning our stance in life, our position, our sense of identity and power are represented in bone. This can be especially significant if imprints happen when bone is forming and growing.

Much of the information we received as young children was accepted as a given. We took it as the truth without question and without resistance. This includes our parents' view of the world, their religion, and their belief systems. It includes our ancestral history and cultural heritage. Since we accept these things as true, there is no resistance to their imprinting. The stronger or more repetitive of these views lodge in the bone. And because of the density of the bone, they tend to be firmly placed and long lasting.

Injunctions from our parents or other authority figures tend to go into the bone. If you were repeatedly told that you were a beautiful child, smart, extra-special, the light of your parent's lives, and believed it, those beliefs will be lodged in your bones and have a resonance in your life.

A dear friend of mine contracted a mild case of polio as a child. In the course of recovery, her grandmother held her a great deal, touched and stroked her skin, all the while telling her how beautiful and talented she was. Since my friend received this nurturing/affirming attention from the grandmother without resistance, she accepted that she was beautiful and talented. Her very bones received this information. As an adult, this woman is one of the most talented, secure, and self-directed people I know. I attribute a substantial part of this to the deep impact of the grandmother's attention.

If, on the other hand, you were told repeatedly and let yourself believe, that you were stupid, dumb, and clumsy, then that too would go into the bone and affect who you are. Truths are bone deep.

Issues of shamein bone are found in bone. "You should be ashamed of yourself!" says the authority figure; and it goes right to the bone. The child doesn't question whether shame is really appropriate; he is just ashamed.

Early childhood lossesin bone often go into the bone. The loss of a parent through death or divorce is huge to the child. Even the loss of a pet or favorite doll or toy can be significant to the child. A difficult, traumatic divorce will evoke feelings of loss and guilt, and impact the bone. Of course some divorces may actually be a blessing for the child, and when skillfully done, may leave no significant imprint.

Zero Balancing experience has shown that these early childhood losses are often held rather specifically in the lower rib cage. The ribs are so intimately connected with the lungs that this observation is consistent with the acupuncture teaching that grief and loss are associated with the lungs. When I encounter a person with a history of an early loss, especially if it still evokes an emotional response, I carefully palpate and evaluate ribs 7, 8, 9, and 10. There are different ways that bone-held grief or loss may feel to the fingers. I palpate for devitalization, flatness, dullness, or the lack of resilience caused by the numbness of a severe shock. I palpate for energetic fragility of bone, which feels similar to thin or delicate china.

Common figures of speech indicate other types of experience that go to the bone level. Sometimes when you overwork you get such a deep tiredness that you are "bone tired" or "tired to the bone." In a relationship you may be "hurt to the quick." Not only do these expressions indicate the depth of the experience, but they also indicate a folk-knowledge that the bone is our deepest level of body feelings.

Most of us develop childhood strategies of one sort or another. It is very common to find these strategies or behavioral patterns held in the skeleton as posture, head positions or ways of using the body. Some of those strategies serve us well. Others are useful as children, but later in life do not serve us. Some may never have been helpful to us from the beginning. To the extent that we can release any held patterns that no longer serve us, we can reduce recurrent stimuli that reinforce outdated behavior.

At a workshop some years ago I did a ZB with a thirty-year-old man. He had no physical complaints. His main concern was a feeling of insecurity, particularly in terms of relationships. The first half moon traction I did on his legs revealed marked bowing of the energy configuration in both legs. The finding of bowed leg energy is not unusual, but the intensity I found here led me to query further about his past history. He had grown up on a cattle ranch in South America and had been horseback riding as long as he could remember. During his teens he learned to ride bulls, where he needed to grip with his legs to stay on the animal for any length of time. His history was fully consistent with the marked bowed energy in his legs. By the end of the session the feeling of the bowed energy in the legs was 70-80 per cent improved. His walking looked more grounded and secure than before the session.

I have no idea what happened to this young man after the workshop, but my experience over the years leads me to believe that on both the physical and energetic levels his legs will now give him the kinesthetic experience of being better grounded and more stable. This literal security could spill over into his life generally, including relationships.

Finding some bowing of the energy body in the legs is not an uncommon finding. It is a common pattern in children who have stood on the outside edges of their feet. We saw this in the session I did on Sara. This habit is often the result of insecurity in a child, and reflects a strategy of not taking a firm stand. It may be in both legs or in one leg only. Experience with many people has shown that these patterns can be reduced or overcome with the use of clearer, stronger fields of energy through the extremities, which frequently results in more secure, less guarded behavior.

A person can receive a trauma, even as severe as a fracture, and heal well with little or no residual effect. This is particularly true if the person is psychologically stable and/or well tended at the time of the trauma. It may just represent one of life's events without causing discordant vibration or a psychological aftermath.

If a person is emotionally unstable at the time of trauma it can become problematic for the person. Imagine a child, six years old. The mother goes shopping, and tells the child not to ride her bike while she is gone. After the mother leaves, the child does ride her bike, falls, and breaks an arm. The mother gets home to find a child who is in pain, injured, and feeling guilty for disobeying. "See what happens when you don't obey me, when you don't listen! God is punishing you!" The child feels that neither the parent nor God love her. She has offended them both. That injunction is superimposed on top of rejection, pain, guilt, anger, and physical pain. These messages can all fuse together. Even though the bone may be well set and heal completely, an energetic charge or imprint can remain and have long-lasting effects. The feeling of being punished by God is especially deep and may well persist into adulthood, with whatever implication that may have for the person. It certainly could affect spiritual maturity. I am reminded of a particularly fine book, *Healing Your Rift With God,* by Paul Sibcy, which looks at deep, often forgotten, issues of this sort.

Imprinting into the level of bone tends to happen in situations where we take in information that we accept as the truth, without reaction or challenge. It tends to happen when there is a strong emotional charge that takes the vibration all the way through soft tissue defenses. Imprinting also goes to bone when the bone itself is involved with trauma or accident.

A distortion of bone vibration at the point(s) of origin or insertion of a muscle may cause a muscle to be tense. The altered bone tension itself can be a feedback loop for chronic dysfunction of the muscle. In therapy, if you encounter muscle tension or spasm that does not respond to your therapy as you would expect, or where muscle tension recurs for no seeming cause, look to the bone itself at the point of muscle attachment. Often that portion of the bone is holding an excess of vibration. Release the excess vibration in the bone via a stronger local tension and the muscle problem frequently releases. This may happen without even touching the body of the muscle itself.

Soft Tissue

Memory, emotions, and stress involve soft tissue differently than bone. In addition to the inherent movement possible in soft tissue, the autonomic nervous system directly translates our mental and emotional life to organs and soft tissue. This is one key to understanding psychosomatic medicine. As a result of this connection with the nervous system, much of our personal history and the stress of day-to-day living are reflected in tissues and organs. Ulcers, hypertension, or skin rashes are only a few of many possible examples.

In the traditional Chinese five element model of medicine there is a very different yet specific relationship between emotions and organs: anger is related to the liver and gallbladder; joy, or the lack of joy, to the heart and small intestines; sympathy to the spleen, pancreas and stomach; grief to the lungs and large intestine; and fear to the kidney and bladder. According to this model, each of us is identified with one or more of these elements and their emotion/organ complexes, and in a sense we are predestined to interact with vibration in certain ways. Under stress we have a propensity for certain emotional expression or organ dysfunction. Knowing a person's strengths and weaknesses in relation to the five elements gives us strong clues as to where to look for, and how to deal with, held vibration within that person.

Acupuncture meridian anatomy suggests where we might find vibrations stored in soft tissue. For example, the gallbladder meridian runs through the pelvis, hips, and down the outside of the legs. Tension found in these areas is often related to emotions associated with the gallbladder, issues of anger, frustration, and/or blocked creativity. The pathway of the gallbladder also passes through the jaw, and as we know, jaw tension is frequently related to determination, frustration, or anger.

Many behavioral patterns lodge in soft tissue. A person who grew up in an authoritarian environment often has a limited backward glide of the neck. Conditioned to stand at attention, a person can lock the neck straight, which limits the posterior glide. The most frequent examples of an authoritarian environment include a military family, a military school, a strongly religious family, or a Catholic school or convent. When I find significant posterior glide restriction I often ask if the person was raised in an authoritarian environment. He may reply in amazement, "How did you know that?" If the authoritarian background doesn't pertain, the second most common cause of posterior glide restriction is that of an accident to the neck or upper back.

Background Field

Vibrations may be held in the background field. These vibrations come from any number of sources, the most obvious being from life events in which we had some personal involvement. An important but less obvious source is vibration that surrounds us but which has not been generated by our own actions. I call these "non-self" vibrations. Although most of these peripheral vibrations just pass by and have no effect on us, under certain circumstances they can impress on our field. Frequently these vibrations locate in our background field.

Not Us

One example of non-self vibrations can involve the nine-month period of fetal gestation. The fetus is totally dependent on the environment provided by the mother. It is well known that the fetus is directly affected by the blood chemistry of the mother. We see warnings posted that alcoholic consumption during pregnancy may cause developmental abnormalities in the child. "Crack" babies can be born with addictions. A person can be sensitized to tobacco when the mother smoked during pregnancy.

Less obvious are the effects on the fetus from the vibration existing within the amniotic fluid. For nine months the developing child is immersed in a sea of fluid. This amniotic fluid holds a vibration, which is a reflection of the fetus, the mother, and tangential influences. The fetus has no way of discerning what vibration belongs

to the developing self, what belongs to the mother, and what belongs to other influences.

Assume a mother is chronically depressed. The vibration of the
amniotic fluid will reflect this depression. For months her developing fetus is immersed in this field and to the extent that the fluid vibration reflects the depressed emotion, the fetus may begin to resonate and be entrained by it. After birth a tendency to depression
will most likely pervade this person's life. The person will consider
it as his or her own norm, even though the vibration actually belongs to the mother. In truth it is a non-self vibration and not the
person's true disposition.

I have chosen the example of depression associated with gestation because the amniotic fluid is an obvious field in which the fetus
is immersed. But this could be true with any field surrounding us
that contains an impressionable vibration. If the circumstances are
right they can affect us and imprint patterns of feelings and behavior that are not actually who we really are.

Removing non-self vibrations

Non-self vibrations can be lessened or removed in a number of ways
including touch, mental activity, ritual, and others. Surprisingly,
this is often not difficult to accomplish. For example while treating a
woman who is chronically depressed I learn that her mother was
depressed throughout the pregnancy. With the client supine, I can
raise the vibratory frequency of her fields through the use of touch,
which would loosen the contents of the fields. The exact technique
to raise vibratory fields will be described in Chapter 10. When this
amplified vibration is established, I would lift up the whole cage,
and ask her to bring any of her mother's vibrations into her field
that don't belong to her. I would then instruct her to drop into my
hands as she lets go of these non-self vibrations. The simultaneous
experience of her body dropping while she herself is mentally dropping things away promotes the release of the non-self vibration.

Several factors help make this process work: first that the
mother was actually depressed during the pregnancy and that the
vibration was transmitted to the fetus; second, that the client has
accepted the possibility that some vibrations may not be hers and
that it is possible to release them; and, third, that it is clearly

framed that the purpose of the session is to release non-self vibrations. Proof of the effectiveness of this process would be the lessening of depression and this would show up over time.

I have worked releasing non-self vibrations with a number of people, and have seen subsequent changes occur in both feeling and behavior. Does everyone respond? No. Do a number of people seem better? Yes. Can a person be totally freed from these early influences? "Totally" is too big a word, but time and again I have seen lasting effects from this approach.

Whenever you suspect that there is a vibration present within a person that is not part of who they really are, it is possible to release it or lessen its effect by following the ideas presented above. This possibility will be further explored when we discuss alchemical fulcrums in Chapter 10.

Modeling

Another example of non-self vibration occurs through modeling of behavior. Children naturally tend to model their external environment: they imitate what they see around them, how their parents stand, how they parents interact, how they talk, how friends behave, and how the people close to them respond to stressful situations. These non-verbal influences can come in through any channel and, while not part of one's birth destiny, can affect our internal program of who we will become.

When I was young my great aunt lived with us for several years. She had Parkinsonism and was confined to a wheel chair. I remember the revulsion I had whenever I looked at her, and, later, whenever I saw a person who reminded me of her. Years later in my medical practice I set about removing this program. In my visits to convalescent hospitals, whenever I would feel this sense of revulsion, I made it a practice to stop and communicate with the individual involved, developing a sense of compassion rather than judgment. Over time I became emotionally neutral in situations that reminded me of my aunt, and felt that I had overridden or released the early impressions I had taken on.

Aka

There are flows of energy that extend from us to other people or events, which is in a sense extraneous to who we are. One of the best descriptions of this idea is found in the Hawaiian Huna tradition, which describes a concept of "aka." Aka is dense psychic energy, so dense that you can almost feel it. This type of energy can attach us to something or someone. A classic example of this is a gift given "with strings attached." The giver has a lot of expectations around the outcome of giving the gift. He or she may expect something back or may be manipulating the receiver toward a desired end. It is not a true gift, in the sense that some compensation is expected. We could say that the gift has a lot of aka.

Aka shows up in many places. Assume your daughter goes to college and you don't truly separate from her, wishing strongly, or secretly, that she weren't going. This condition of the relationship can produce a dense psychic string or cord between you. These connections or strings are real, though unseen, and can affect the subsequent behavior of both parties.

Aka connections are often limiting to self and others, and they usually form without our full awareness. If you can't let go of an old relationship within a reasonable period of time, for example, there may be a lot of aka in or around the relationship. The aka connections will limit your ability to resolve the relationship and to form a new one. If a new relationship does form, without the release of aka, it may be more confused or difficult than it need be.

There may be strong aka connections with loved ones who have died. Long after a reasonable grieving period, strong emotions may persist around the death.

Aka can be released or lessened in a number of ways. Connections can be released through ritual, visualization, meditation, and other activities that have a direct connection to energy. For example, to help resolve a relationship, you could picture yourself and your ex-partner each having a clear field with no attachments to one another. Or you might pass your hand in front of your body with conscious attention to release or break any aka strings. For connections too strong or dense to be released by these simple procedures, a more powerful ritual or practice is needed.

Archetypal Vibration of Emotions

I believe that part of our emotional response to life results from our interaction with the literal movement of energy. From this viewpoint we respond to the form which vibration is taking at any given moment, and not just to the event causing the vibration. I call such a response archetypal.

The Webster's dictionary defines an archetype as "the original pattern or model after which a thing is made, a model or first form, a prototype." Energy has a form or pattern as it moves or is held stationary, and we respond specifically to that configuration. We literally respond to the pattern of the energy that has been evoked by some event. Just as when we sit in a boat riding the waves, we respond to the field we are in.

Energy can rise and fall, or become dispersed, separated, blocked, collapsed, twisted, or jammed, to name some possible configurations. Each of these configurations can cause a different emotional response or emotional tone. For instance, energy that is suddenly blocked provokes the response of frustration or anger. Energy that thins as two objects move apart provokes loss and accompanying feelings of sadness. I call these emotions and reactions "archetypal" because they are in response to the configuration of the vibration and not to the substance of the event itself.

Archetypal anger   Archetypal loss

Following energy that suddenly expands we frequently experience shame or embarrassment as we return to our usual way of being. Assume that you are in a group circle where people are asked to introduce themselves. People take their turn. As your turn approaches internal tension usually builds. When your time finally comes you make your statement to the whole group from a heightened state of vibration. When your turn is over your heightened energy field drops as you settle into yourself, and it often swings below the baseline. A sense of shame, inadequacy, or embarrassment is often associated with this period where the energy is low. How well we know this experience!

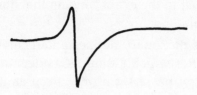

Archetypal rise and fall of energy

This need not be a problem if you realize that part of your response is due to the archetypal drop of energy. Your feelings are not all personal, but rather represent a response to the fall of tension or vibration in the field. If you understand this sequence and were to feel embarrassed, all you have to do is to sit for a short period and just let the feelings pass as the energy reforms. You just ride the wave without taking it personally. Shortly the emotion is gone, and you feel fine, never having allowed the reactive feelings and emotions to engage your consciousness. You have been the observer of the energy movement and have stayed free of emotion, like the cork floating on a turbulent sea.

If, on the other hand, you don't understand this archetypal movement and believe that you are the full cause of the emotions, you may experience shame for hours as you process the feelings. And if your personal history has already sensitized you to feelings of shame or embarrassment, you could really become overwhelmed with self-recrimination. Your inner critic may have a field day demeaning the performance of your brief presentation. Many of your old feelings of insufficiency would arise and could ruin your whole day.

It is so important to realize that part of what we feel may not fully be ours. If we don't separate the archetypal reaction from the personal one, an archetypal response can lead us into unnecessary pain and struggle. A sudden startled reaction may evoke fear; but this doesn't mean that you are a timid or fearful person. It's a natural reaction. Knowing this you can just experience the fear and then let it go by. If you think the fear is all yours, it may present ongoing problems for some time.

A different type of archetypal response is seen with the roller-coaster experience. The car goes into the steep descent and people scream. The descent is so sharp that energy rushes into the field and overloads it. There is a need to release this charge and hence the scream. Some of it is therefore archetypal and not necessarily just a scream of fear.

Body functions themselves are affected by shifts of energy. You may have diarrhea when nervous, or you could be constipated if your body needs to conserve energy. The release or conservation of energy can simply be the body's response to maintain homeostasis. This may also be true of some sneezes, coughs, and skin rashes. A number of body responses are situational and not pathological, and should be allowed to run their course and not be medicated. Of course, if a symptom or change in body function continually repeats, it does need to be evaluated for underlying pathology.

Closing

The imprinting of memory, emotion, and experience on the energy fields of the body seems to be part of the human condition, as well as the body's response to excess, deficiency, or movement of energy and vibration. I have shown a number of ways in which I believe these happen. What is important about these ideas is that they open doors to new ways of understanding and altering our internal environment, and thereby directly and naturally affect the health and well being for ourselves and others.

Chapter Eight

Zero Balancing Session with John

Fritz: Good morning, John. I look forward to doing a Zero Balancing Session with you. Is there anything particular you want to work with?

John: This morning I decided I would like to frame a ZB session around who I actually am, as opposed to who I think I am. It has been a tumultuous couple of years for me because I've focused on how things "ought to be," instead of accepting how they actually are.

My daughter just had a baby, and my parents are old and will be dying soon. It's a very big transition time for me and my family as the generations shift. I'm taking up a new role in life and I would like to begin from a place of authenticity, rather than pretending. That would be good.

Fritz: John, I would like to frame the ZB in two parts. In the first part of the session let's bring clearer fields of energy through your body-mind to release unnecessary mental activity. Then, let's move from the level of ego—the experience of duality thinking and ego-based referencing—to the experience of oneness with yourself. On the level of oneness you are beyond or outside duality, beyond struggle, and either in, or closer to, the level of spirit. Instead of referencing the two, and keeping yourself in that mind-ego struggle, you go to the one, which is who you are. The essence of the ZB will first be to clarify the two and then seek the one; to help you move from two to one.

Fritz begins the ZB by stepping behind John to evaluate the shoulder girdle. Before picking up the arm he pauses.

Fritz: I was going to say, "Let's invite our guides," but on deeper reflection I think that encouraging external references might confuse the issue we are working on. So let it be you and me, and we'll leave the guides just watching.

John: Well, they brought me here.

Fritz continues, and then with a hand on John's left shoulder:

Fritz: I can well remember situations of not knowing who I am, what I really want to do, or want to happen. To get beneath the confusion of the ego, I have—and occasionally still do—flip a coin. I'd define the issue, "Shall I go to the movie or not? Heads I do, tails I don't." I'd flip the coin, carefully observing my first feeling reaction to the outcome. That was closer to the truth than was the designation of the coin face. If it was tails—don't go to the movie—and my first reaction was disappointment—"Darn, I really want to go"—I'd go. *(laughter)* This would get me beneath my confusion and help me discover my true desire. I needed to trick myself for a long time before I got beneath the conditioning of 'ought' and 'should.'

Fritz then goes to evaluate the right side of the shoulder girdle.

Fritz: To help you get out of your mind, just let me have your arm, so you're free.

John lets go with a deep breath and gives control of his arm to Fritz. As he lifts the left arm, Fritz again asks John to let him have the arm as he begins to move it in a circular pattern. Another deep exhale from John.

After Fritz evaluates the shoulder girdle, then the pelvic girdle, he asks John to lie on his back. Fritz gives him a long half moon fulcrum through the legs. He then does a fulcrum into the feet and holds the heels for an extended time, as if tuning into John's interior.

Fritz: Part of this ZB will be to help you locate a point of reference within yourself. That point won't be the mind. It won't be the shoulders, hips, hands, or feet because these are involved with external world interaction. The reference point needs to be within you, near or at your center of gravity. You need to find it. The point needs to be free of duality; therefore singular, not bilateral. It will be somewhere in the exact midline of your body, probably somewhere in the pelvis.

Fritz then moves to work on John's lower back. Making a good connection on both sides, he adds:

I remember you once told me of your early history and of not having enough food as an infant—a conditioning of not having enough. The fear of scarcity—like all fears—is rooted in duality. When you connect with a singular reference point you will depart duality and the fear will drop away.

Again, John, you don't have to do any thinking during the ZB. Just be aware of the feelings in your body and enjoy yourself.

Fritz evaluates the sacroiliac joints through the pelvic motions. He puts fulcrums to the sacroiliac and right inguinal ligament. He palpates across the abdomen. He then begins to put fulcrums into the dorsal hinge and lumbar area of the back. Working signs are in evidence as John's eyeballs move back and forth beneath the closed lids. He smiles . . . and smiles . . . and smiles.

Fritz: Can you share what's happening?

John: I just know it feels very good. I don't know quite what's going on. *(pause)* I think the energy in my right side is building, but I don't want to get too heady about it.

Fritz: There is tension along the second, third, and fourth lumbar vertebrae, on the right-hand side, where I'm putting in the fulcrums. It's an area of holding. *(Fritz then checks the pelvic motions by gently pressing on the anterior iliac spines.)* That's much better.

John nods approvingly, and then lets go into the sensation as his head lolls to the left. He licks his lips and continues to smile. We wait.

Fritz (to everyone): My sense is that deep nurturing is occurring. The vibration that was held in those three vertebrae has been released, and is now recycling back into John's overall field of energy. It is feeding him on a very deep level. It's probably feeding him in the same period of life when scarcity began, when he was very young. He's being fed at the time of his first month, second month, or even his first day. This is a very primal moment.

John: That's right! *John nods.*

Fritz: As this feeds you, keep letting it into the pelvis. As the energy builds, let it build there.

John lets out a breath and says something imperceptible to Fritz. Fritz touches his lower abdomen and says, "You feel it in here." John nods — smiling happily. Fritz then returns to work under the back, and John says that he feels a release from the shoulder. Fritz replies simply: "You don't have to do it all." He then moves under John's right leg and puts fulcrums in the right hip, pelvis, and then the acetabular ridge. John lets out a breath with a gasp. Fritz checks: "Too much?" "No. It's great," comes the reassurance. Fritz goes again to the acetabular ridge and says:

Fritz: Remember, all this is coming from you. This is all you.

Fritz then moves to the left leg and puts fulcrums on the other side, focusing on the acetabular ridge. More sighs.

John: "Very, very good!"

Fritz: Keep letting the sensation — the vibration — come into the pelvis. Let it build.

John: That's exactly what it's doing. It's building and circulating faster and faster...

Fritz: Good. Keep the energy there.

Fritz then moves a bolus of energy down the gallbladder meridian of John's left leg, which initiates various gasps of "Wow" and "Delicious." John indicates his pelvis, and says that the pressure is building there. Fritz acknowledges this and goes on to put a single fulcrum in John's left foot. John laughs softly.

Fritz: Keep it in the pelvis.

John: It wants to go straight out.

Fritz: Keep it in the pelvis

John: Aww...

Fritz: ... for a while

John: Ohh. All right.

A double fulcrum to the right foot extracts another "Wooah" of pleasure from John. Fritz then moves up to John's head.

Fritz: How are you doing?

John: Wonderful. It sank lower in the pelvis that time. It feels great.

Fritz: Good for you!

Fritz then proceeds to work on John's upper back. He evaluates the neck and works the neck muscles. Going under the rib cage, he raises John's whole upper back off the table, suspended in space. John relaxes into Fritz's fingers and his smile is replaced by a look of deep relaxation. Deep breaths follow. Fritz disconnects, and then, returning to the thoracic spine, he again raises John's back on his fingers

Fritz: I'd like you to drop away any residues of fear from your body.

John: Ooohh! Man. It's like lights are turning on.

Fritz: Just let the residue drop away. You're secure. You're safe. Occasionally bring your attention into your pelvis, and feel how stable, how full, how delicious it feels. *(pause)* That's it, get your reference down there.

John: There's a bit a fear right in the middle of it.

Fritz: Let it go, you don't need any fear there.

John: Yaaay!

Fritz: When it's gone, fill those spaces with a new vibration. Take a few deep breaths into them. Bring your center right into the pelvis. Identify and fill that space.

John breathes deeply, repeatedly.

Fritz: Once again, see if there is any fear left in the pelvis, and if so, let it drop away; especially fear from the period of your early childhood. *(long pause)* Did you get the fear out of the pelvis?

John: It left a mark where it was. I don't think it's there anymore, but I can still feel where it was.

Fritz: Stay in the space where it was, and begin to breathe new light into that area. Let the vibration of light heal that scar.

John: Yes, that's what it is, a scar.

Fritz: I'd like no residue in the pelvis.

Fritz then moves his hands to the very top of John's shoulders, and seems to direct energy down John's body. An exquisite smile appears on John's face and his left finger and thumb connect together as his left hand makes a slow dance away from the couch. As his hand returns to his chest,

John lets out a long, relaxed breath. Fritz disconnects, pauses, and then makes another suggestion.

Fritz: John, are you willing to reclaim any personal power you may have lost, or perhaps have never acknowledged? *(pause)* Your Spirit power. *(John nods his head)* As you do this, feel it in your pelvis.

John's hands connect to his pelvis and his eyes repeatedly open for a short time and then slowly close.

Fritz: It's like reclaiming your own identity.

John: Yes.

The sun suddenly comes into the room, and the group acknowledges the synchronicity. A long period of silence and profundity fill the room. Time stops. Eventually John lets out a very long breath. Fritz wipes across the top of John's shoulders, and rubs and reworks above and below the upper rib cage.

Fritz: I am getting ready to close the session. Is there anything else you would like me to do? We are in no rush.

John: No, I don't need anything but I do have a question. I have a deep awareness here *(he points to his pelvis)* and it feels great. But I've also got quite a strong sensation here *(points to his stomach)* I don't know whether to come up into it, or come down from it or to leave it alone, or what to do. That's all.

Fritz: Keep taking it all down to the pelvis. Energy can rise in the body in two ways: it can come up through the body in a general manner, from the pelvis and abdomen, through the diaphragm, the heart area and up into the neck and head; or it can come up from the floor of the pelvis, through the sushumna (the central channel in the spine), to the top of the head. I'd keep the charge in the pelvis and let it climb its way out, through the sushumna, in its own time.

The desired outcome is a self-referencing system into your own spirit, which is going to be located centrally in your pelvis, near your personal center of gravity.

John: Okay. Got it.

Fritz then finishes the session with an integrating fulcrum to John's neck, and closing fulcrums in the thoracic cage, and on the pelvis. He concludes with a half moon vector through the legs, integrating the whole body. He then presses on the soles of John's feet and says:

Fritz: You can breathe a little lower. *(John does so, and something shifts internally.)* There you go. As you come back to full consciousness, be aware of being fully nurtured, free of fear, very powerful, self-referenced low in the pelvis, and at home in your own center of gravity.

John: Down below, yes. Not way up here *(pointing towards his head).*

Fritz: Correct. That's why you've been caught in all these tangles; the center of gravity — your center of reference — has been too high in the body. Stay in the pelvis.

John: Yes. Yes. It's that old thing. You travel round the whole world, and the secret's on your doorstep.

They both laugh.

Fritz: You discover it right here, below the navel.

More laughter.

John then walks up and down by the couch. He looks much stronger and more solid; more empowered. Even his voice is deeper and stronger. His walk has purpose to it.

John's report of the ZB experience

Sitting on the couch, talking to Fritz before the session started, I was aware of a slight awkwardness. He accepted what I wanted from the session, and made some comments which showed me he understood exactly what I meant. But he also said a couple of things which led me to wonder if there was something inadequate — or worse, phony — about what I had said. It wasn't what he said; more a slight feeling of being in the wrong. I didn't worry about it at the time, because I absolutely trusted Fritz's goodwill; later, I realized it was a typical pattern for me — going back to early childhood.

When he put his hands on my back, I was immediately reassured. It felt so safe, so accepting, and so empowering to have that solid presence behind me. He was behind me in all senses of the phrase. However, my awkwardness returned when he evaluated the movement of my shoulders. I noticed that although I wanted to let go and allow him to do the work, a bit of me was retaining control of parts of the movement. I felt awkward about not surrendering. Then I felt awkward when he suggested I let go. Then I felt awkward that I wouldn't be able to do it. Then I felt awkward as he started the evaluation again, and I could feel I was still holding on.

But somehow I did let go. It was quite a relief; and I knew that it had set the scene for the rest of the session.

The first half moon fulcrum felt good but I felt very stuck. There was no flow in my body—no graceful, easy, responsive movement. Then Fritz started to work quite hard and repeatedly on my right lower back. It was very pleasurable; I really enjoyed it. I felt myself getting lighter and lighter, and I felt a release from my right shoulder, as if I was dropping a burden. Then he worked on my hip and buttocks on that side and I started to feel a concentration of energy in my pelvic bowl. It was swirling and powerful, and increased in intensity all the time. Again, very pleasurable.

When he worked with my foot, I felt the energy rise from my pelvic bowl up my spine in two waves, crisscrossing between each vertebra. It was exquisite. But at some point he said, or I remembered he had said, that it was better to keep the energy in the pelvic area. I was reluctant to do so, but I knew it would be stupid to have a very experienced guide and not take his advice; so I put my attention back into that area, and lo and behold the energy returned there as obediently as if it had been on a lead. From then on, through all the rest of the work on the lower half of my body, there continued to be a strong increase of energy in the pelvic area. Each touch seemed much stronger than the last—on the borderline of pain and pleasure—and boosted the sensation of dynamic movements there.

When Fritz moved to the upper half of my body and asked me how I was doing I was aware that my voice was much deeper and firmer than it had ever been before. This was linked to the growing strength in the pelvic area. As he worked, quite vigorously, I suddenly realized that the vortices had slowed down and become more stable. I now felt heavy in my abdomen and light in my chest. It felt great. I realized that all my life I had thought it was the other way round, but it felt so much better to be solid below and light on top. "Of course," I thought, "the lungs should be light."

Later, when I thought the session was nearly finished and I was feeling very satisfied, Fritz suggested I see if there was fear at any specific location in my body. It was astonishing. Little colored lights went on immediately, like on one of those old "Find your way round the city" maps, where you pressed a button and pinpoint lights showed the location of cinemas, or—at the press of another button—tube stations. As he directed me to do so, I let go of fear from all these locations. It was easy. I did it quickly. Then, as I checked again, I got a shock. There was a large deep fear I hadn't noticed before, right in the middle of my abdomen; right in the middle of the area I thought was now so strong and energized. It was like discovering that the head of the CIA was a Soviet spy.

Slowly, slowly, the fear went, but it left something behind. I wasn't quite sure what, but it was a pain of some sort, extending to the left about three inches from the mid-line. I didn't quite know what to do with it. Then Fritz suggested that it was a scar. Exactly! That was it. He told me to heal it completely so that there was no trace of it left. I found this difficult, partly because I couldn't find a method of doing so. Finally I got it. I sort of blended or melted the two sides of the scar together at a deep level and then brushed over the surface as you might brush fresh glossy paint over a surface crack. At the same time I found that, involuntarily, my left hand was slowly and delicately pulling away from the area; as if, I thought after a minute or two, it was removing a thread which had stitched up the wound. It took a long time but finally my left hand dropped away and there was no trace of the scar in my abdomen. Then I felt better still; very solid and well.

Through all this I felt present and clear—a bit of surprise. I opened my eyes a couple of times and I was alert and very conscious of everything that was happening. It was the same when got off the couch. I didn't feel in the least spaced out or "floaty." On the contrary, I walked easily in a very grounded way. My knees were bent and I placed my feet slowly and deliberately—not ponderously, though, but with a lovely flowing movement. My voice was deep and resonant—normally it is quite light and nasal—and it matched my walk.

I have had the idea before of moving and speaking from the center of me, from my pelvic bowl, but I had never had the experience before. I felt so much better now. It felt like a fresh start in life.

Chapter Nine

Zero Balancing Session with Alan

Fritz: Hello, Alan. Is there's anything special you care to work with? Any particular issues you'd like to put into the field?

Alan: In terms of my body, I have a feeling in my neck, as if I've been on a long flight, or in a strange bed, as if I've slept awkwardly. On my left side there is something that I can't untangle, I can't even touch it through the muscle. But I know that when I move my neck something's not quite free.

Fritz: How long has that been with you? Weeks, months?

Alan: A month. I've started doing exercise more regularly. My body is really enjoying it, but it may be that I have aches and pains as a result of that.

Fritz: Anything else?

Alan: When I overload, my weakness goes into a cough. A sort of dry cough, deficient of energy. It has been worse recently. I have been with people who have been grieving the loss of a family member. I naturally empathize with them, and perhaps I began to resonate with them and felt too personally what was going on—like blending with their grief and emotion.

Fritz: Be careful with your boundaries. If they are suffering loss, don't blend with that. At interface you stay clear and can be a support for them, without necessarily ...

Alan: Taking it on.

Fritz: Yes.

Alan: Otherwise I feel good and in good spirits.

Fritz: Great. *(to everyone)* In terms of Zero Balancing working strategies there are always a number of things to consider. The fact that Alan can't quite locate the problem in his neck alerts me to the fact that it may not be all physical, and/or that there may be another end of a string somewhere in the body, which is holding his neck out of balance. I assume the neck evaluation will give me specific information. Likewise evaluation of the energetics of the rib cage will give information as to whether there is block or deficient energy. At this stage we don't know.

Alan: This morning we talked about fields, and the possibility of a fetus picking up emotions or conditioning from its mother through vibrations in the amniotic fluid. My father died when my mother was in her third month of pregnancy. A shocking death. I'm very conscious that something happened. It was totally unexpected. I am not sure what effect this shock and loss had on me at that time, and whether it is, or could be, one of my current issues.

Fritz: These early major events certainly can imprint lastingly and deeply. I have known you for a long time, and my sense is that you have worked through the loss of your father quite well. Over the years it has motivated you to look deep within yourself, and has been one of the stimuli for your spiritual journey.

Alan: From knowing my brother, and from talking to my mother, I know that she was holding him and was pregnant with me, while being a nurse in the Blitz. Many times she did not know whether she was going to live or die, because bombs were coming down, but she would just continue working and then go down into the bomb shelters. The power of that clearly set something up in my brother—fear and anger and such things.

Fritz: It is certainly hard when a baby gets caught up in such things. It has no understanding or defense against it. The child can only react to these stimuli.

Alan: I am a war baby. I've just been to a number of fifty-year anniversaries and the whole trauma has come back into my field of awareness again. I still feel as if I'm a part of the war.

Fritz: When we're working I'll look for any vibrations from the war, and particularly for vibrations you may be holding from your mother and her experience of the sudden loss of your father. These vibrations would not really be yours — they were hers. Of course I will also look at your neck discomfort, the chest cough, and deficient lung qi. Anything else?

Alan: *(He smiles broadly)* I'm totally open.

Fritz moves behind Alan, places his hand on Alan's right shoulder and begins evaluating the movements and energetics of the shoulder girdle. While doing this Fritz talks to the audience.

Fritz *(to everyone):* When you begin to work with someone it is important to determine the general level of mind/body clarity in order to ascertain whether a specific restriction, limitation, or block is relevant to the session. Your clarity about this helps determine the degree of sensitivity that you'll need to read and thus interpret their problems. With Alan I am finding that his body and vibratory fields are very organized and clear. This is consistent with his *tai chi*, his internal practices, and his general life style. Alan is also a ZB practitioner, and as I have mentioned elsewhere, people who perform Zero Balancing tend to become clearer themselves just from doing the work on others.

He has clear fields. So as I assess and evaluate, I will fine tune my senses as one does when looking for a needle in a haystack. When people are basically clear, you hunt for that hidden place where energy or structure is compromised, or, knowing that much of the past history has been cleared, you pay particular attention to what is available at this moment in time. It may end up that there are only a few places where we will be working, which enhances the power of each area.

When a person does not have a clear body/mind, or has numerous problems, then you don't look so deeply, but rather take off one layer or one level evenly over the body/mind. Each fulcrum may be less powerful in its own right, but the accumulated effect is very powerful and effective.

Fritz (turning his attention to Alan): Here, as I'm reading the movement of your left shoulder, I'm finding that somewhere the shoulder girdle is locking. This is probably tied up to the neck and may be one of the strings I am looking for. I'm not yet sure, but am going to include it as a possibility.

Alan: I dislocated my left shoulder some eighteen months ago.

Fritz (clearly remembering): That's right! Part of it could be from that, but I remember checking your shoulder several months ago, and I recall it being freer than it is at this moment. My guess is that something more is going on, which could just be life stuff, or something more specific around your friend's loss. In any case, be present in the moment and let the stress of the last few weeks drop away.

Alan: Thank you.

Fritz finishes the sitting assessments of the shoulder girdle and the pelvic girdle and Alan lies down on his back, further relaxing into the session. After a strong half moon vector through the legs, Fritz moves to evaluate Alan's lower back.

Fritz (to everyone): I'm thinking aloud now. The half moon vector I just did revealed body tension around both scapulae. This sort of tension often results from over-responsibility. With Alan, I'm wondering whether the sense of responsibility around his friend's loss could be lodging there. My suggestion again to Alan is to let go any excess responsibility around his friends' loss; to be a friend but not the responsible party. Specifically, to drop way from the body any excess responsibility that does not serve him.

Alan makes an acknowledging expression.

Fritz (to everyone): Zero Balancing has been influenced by many sources. From the influence of osteopathy has come the importance of evaluation. In ZB we don't balance every area of the body we touch, but primarily those which evaluation has shown to have room for improvement. When we work with a part, we first evaluate the structure and the energetics. If they are well balanced, we move on. If they are compromised, we put in fulcrums. ZB is specific and it is important for the practitioner to have a clear understanding of the fine distinction between an evaluating touch and a balancing touch. You usually only balance where your evaluation indicates a need to balance.

With Alan, it's mostly evaluation. There is one point around the third lumbar vertebra where energy is holding a bit, and another on the upper tip of the right sacroiliac. Everywhere else is clear. ZB is very efficient, very specific, very exact: I just go where I need to go.

Fritz puts in a fulcrum here and there, and then moves on to lift Alan's right leg for an evaluation of the hip joint.

Fritz (to everyone): When you work at the interface of energy and structure, things seem fluid. Like working in clay. Many times it feels like we're actually remodeling or reforming the body/mind. At the boundary of energy and structure, things are alive, moving, plastic, free. When holding the fulcrum, it almost feels like things drop into place, into form. I often get a really beautiful image when I'm working with someone that their whole body/mind is malleable, fluid, and changeable.

Alan: I do feel like I'm made of modeling clay. It's wonderful, such plasticity.

Some chuckles echo around the room.

Fritz (to everyone): We know from quantum physics that particles and waves are interchangeable. They go back and forth. Somewhere there is a point and/or moment in which things can shift and go from form to vibration, or from vibration to form. The secret is to get to that balance point. That's the whole key. When you hold energy and structure in the right relationship, and are dealing with both aspects consciously, then the body seems to move back and forth between them.

Fritz moves energy down the outside of Alan's right leg, along the gallbladder meridian, and Alan lets out a deep breath.

Fritz (to everyone): There are times when I want to work with alchemical fulcrums, those fulcrums of heightened vibration and tension. One way to create such a fulcrum is by addressing the fascia lata along the lateral surface of the thigh; in terms of acupuncture anatomy, this is along the gallbladder meridian. I can move my finger down the outside of the leg, developing a bolus of energy in front of my finger. As I move this bolus through the tissue down the leg, it is doing most of the work rather than my physical finger. I deposit the energy in the bone just above the knee. I can continue this movement down the lower leg beginning just below the knee, at the head of the fibula. I develop another bolus in front of my finger and move it through the soft tissue along the lateral side of the lower leg. I deposit it into the fibula, just below where the body of the muscle begins to form tendon and where you first contact the bone of the fibula. Depositing this energy into the bone will amplify Alan's field. This is working with Alan's own energy under my finger, gathering and concentrating it as I move down the leg, and depositing it back into his body. I am recharging Alan with his own energy. I gather it from one place or one tissue, and circulate it back through another place or tissue—in this case, the bone and skeletal system. He will begin to feel more electric and full as the vibration amplifies and recycles.

Alan's face is flushing as Fritz talks. Fritz then moves to Alan's right foot, evaluates, and creates a fulcrum within the tarsal bones.

Fritz (to everyone): I now have a fulcrum in place. Look at Alan and you can see that he is in a working state. He's not breathing, he's in apnea, he's in stillness. I am holding the fulcrum at the interface of energy and structure and his global body response is that of expanded consciousness. And whenever a person is in an expanded state of consciousness, their mind is extra quiet and it is easier for them to drop deeper into themselves. I suggest to Alan that he allow himself to drop into himself, to let levels of tension just disappear and to go deep into a place of inner calm. Observe Alan as that happens.

Fritz then moves to the left side of the table and evaluates the left hip. The hip and left half of the pelvis are clear. He finds some tension in the bone of the acetabular ridge, where he puts in several fulcrums.

Fritz (to everyone): The acetabular ridge is typically a dense bone because of the recurrent impact of the head of the femur. Within that density it is common to find excess held vibration. In some people this excess charge may hold an emotion, the memory of an event or an attitude. In other cases, such as here, the excess charge is just from the physical impact of recent walking or running. Releasing this for Alan will bring greater clarity to his body, even though it seems that there is no emotional equivalent in the release.

Following the Zero Balancing protocol, Fritz then moves on to check Alan's feet, and then to work with the left foot. He evaluates again, and then places a one-handed fulcrum into the tarsal bones. He completes the work on the lower half of the body by integrating the changes with a half moon vector through both legs.

Fritz: Somewhere there has been a big change in the body energy. I no longer feel that he is holding the excessive responsibility. He is much more here, and much less responsible elsewhere. I think the change is from the accumulated effect of all we have done rather than from any one or two specific fulcrums.

Fritz moves up to the head end of the table, and checks Alan for possible depletion by asking how he is.

Alan (sighs): Hmm. Good. Good.

Fritz evaluates the movement in Alan's neck and his upper back.

Fritz (to everyone): Remember our discussion from the beginning of the session regarding the neck problem, the cough, and the possible deficient energy. In evaluating the neck, I don't find one particular place where the neck is holding, although the movement is not perfect. My guess is that as I release the upper back and left scapula and shoulder area, that the whole neck is going to release. I think the neck is a reflection of something else down in the shoulder girdle.

Fritz continues to work, focusing on Alan's upper back.

Fritz: Regarding the cough and feelings of deficiency, I have the feeling that there is an actual energy deficiency. I think Alan has reached into his resource bank for energy and hasn't replenished it. His tank is running low. Why do I surmise this? Alan's physical body is good, but there is a lack of resilience when I raise up into his rib cage. The lack of resilience is general throughout the thoracic cage as well as specific in the left fourth rib. That rib is holding little charge. We can recharge or replenish by deep fulcrums into the muscles and ribs themselves to release any vibration which is being held. I want to use Alan's own energy for balancing and integration.

Fritz puts a number of deep short fulcrums into the ribs, trapezius muscle, scapula, and shoulder joint, and then integrates them all with a half moon vector to the neck.

Fritz: To further replenish energy, I'm going to put a fulcrum into the whole rib cage, by raising up all the ribs and holding them for ten seconds or so. I will ask Alan to experience the filling of energy. The very fact that he is looking for and having the experience will enhance the movement of his energy which I am releasing. His feeling for it, looking for it, will help draw it in. Ah, there it is. There it is. I am speaking my experience of feeling the in-filling, so that Alan can correlate his experience with mine.

Fritz then goes back to evaluate Alan's neck.

Lots better. Do you see the freedom of that side-bend? We can still gain a bit more, even though it is about 80 percent improved. We haven't yet really worked on the neck itself; we've done all the work below. To see what more I can gain for Alan, I'm going to do one specific neck fulcrum—the half moon vector with a twist, using the second hand. I'll create a half moon vector into the neck as I am rotating the head to the right. Holding this tension with my right hand, with my left hand I'll reach under his neck and contact the right lateral side of his neck with three fingers. Moving medially, I'll develop a bolus of energy in front of my fingers and move the energy through the muscle tissue until I reach the midline of the neck. I'll now repeat this on the other side—it feels so good.

There is a long breath pause.

More and more in my teaching and practice I am emphasizing "letting the body and the mind come together." In theory, we are working on the client's body, asking the mind just to rest while we're working and respond to what we are doing. After a deep fulcrum, or a deep response, however, I'll stop often, stand back, and give the person a moment to experience themselves. Let the mind and the body come together. Alan is now having a moment to himself.

Alan breathes in.

That's the breath; the integrative movement. The mind and the body are now one.

Fritz (to Alan): Are you good?

Alan: Mmm, mmm. *His intonation speaks of a deep calmness.*

Fritz (to everyone): Switching gears, I'll now look for vibrations which may not be Alan's. I'll go back to the full rib cage, using all ten fingers on the ribs, raise up, hold, and open my hands outwards. It's an upwards, opening movement to allow things to release. In doing this, I must ensure that I don't lose any energy that was filled in the rib cage a few moments ago. To prevent energy loss, I will hold him extra firmly during this movement. *The fulcrum is placed and held.*

Fritz (to Alan): Now, let go of any vibrations that don't belong to you, in particular from your time of gestation, and the early war years of your childhood. Just let the vibrations fall away.

Fritz (to everyone after about 15 seconds): My hands are getting tired, so I'll come off. I believe that Alan has already released the vibrations; this usually happens quite quickly. At this moment it is more a matter of him getting used to the new feeling of being without them. He has been so used to these vibrations as being part of him, that without them, there can be a feeling that something is missing. There is a re-acquaintance going on.

Alan's mouth moves a little, as if he is realigning in some way. There is a very slight movement of the right hand. Then, just two, very deep, yet gentle, sighs come from within Alan's body. Fritz continues to watch intensely as the almost imperceptible changes wash over Alan's face and body. Then Fritz, ever so gently, strokes Alan's forehead.

Fritz: I can say to you Alan, because I know you so well, that your father would be very proud of you if he knew you at this moment.

A lengthy period of silence follows, as Alan continues to process the changes going on internally. Fritz continues to watch, and then he moves his hands gently onto Alan's shoulders.

Fritz (to everyone): If a person is working for a long time, I often just touch them to let them know I'm still here; that they are not alone. I'm not interfering with their process; I'm just making a connection, indicating that I am here.

Fritz (to Alan): For your own reality check, open your eyes and get your bearings.

Alan opens his eyes. His eyes blink rapidly to begin with, and then a fixed gaze comes over him. Shortly his eyes look around the ceiling as his conscious control begins to return.

Fritz: I'm now ready to begin to close the session.

Fritz then completes by rapidly going down through Alan's upper and lower back and legs, and finishes with a firm half moon vector to the feet, leaning over the soles of Alan's feet to help ground him.

*As Alan sits up on the couch, his expression is one of joy and alive-
ness, as he sits there with Fritz behind him, rubbing his back. Fritz jokes by
asking Alan to name six presidents of America, or the queens of England,
in order to assure Alan's return to normal waking consciousness. Alan replies "Pre-Boedicea? I am quite present." Fritz states that part of Alan was
"way out there and over-expanded. You really went very, very deep for a
very long time."*

Alan's report of the ZB experience

It was wonderful. You really allowed me to be fully involved in the
session, and that's how I experienced it. In particular, an important
learning for me, was about the experience and use of space. How
rich the time was when I was not being touched and how that space
could be such an integral part of the session. There are so many
parts in this dance: one is when we are being touched; another is
when we are with ourselves and the ZB'er is just holding the space,
without physical touch. It was astonishing.

Chapter Ten

Alchemical Fulcrums

In Zero Balancing it is standard practice to use fulcrums to create fields of vibration stronger than those fields that hold impressions in the body. A fulcrum can act similar to an eraser on a blackboard, where existing marks are removed with a force stronger than the force holding the chalk to the board. This level of fulcrum pressure typically feels familiar to the client, and either feels good or "hurts good." However, there are some fields of tension in the body that are more strongly, deeply, or chronically held, and less or non-responsive to standard fulcrums. A modified force or different strategy, other than simple mechanical pressure, is needed to influence them.

We are all familiar with naturally induced states of altered or expanded consciousness. A wide range of stimuli can precipitate these. At one end of the continuum is high-tension activity such as sports or rock concerts; toward the other end is listening quietly to world-class music or viewing a particular painting. There are many ways to expand consciousness . and transport us to another domain, and, in some cases, even alter our subsequent life.

In my search to find ways of expanding consciousness through touch, I investigated alchemy, shamanism, and ritual. All these domains promote extraordinary experience to provide some special outcome or event.

Exploring Alchemy

Alchemy implies the extraordinary. One definition of alchemy is "any seemingly magical power or process of transmuting." "Transmuting" itself is defined as "changing or altering in form, appearance, or nature, and especially to a higher form." The early alchemists worked to transform base metals into gold. Behind this was the underlying philosophy that if a problem could be reduced to its original state—which they called the *massa confusa*—then it could be re-formed to something of a higher order. The original form needed to be broken down into its fundamental parts and then reconstituted to a higher form. The work was done in a closed container where nothing was added to, nor subtracted from, the original material.

When I read of these alchemical ideas I was struck with the similarities to principals of Zero Balancing. When we look at ZB through the alchemical lens, our desire is to break down an existing form into its basic vibration and release it back into the body. For example, a vibratory configuration held in the body as an idea, belief system, or a traumatic imprint can be released back towards its basic nature of energy or vibration with the use of a fulcrum. In doing this we stay at interface, and work with the person's own energy within their body. We do not attempt to give energy to the person nor take it away.

Exploring Ritual

While investigating alchemy, I realized the complementary nature of ritual to both alchemy and Zero Balancing. This was particularly true of those rituals that were performed to promote change. Assume you want to perform a ritual to break an injunction or belief that you hold. A number of principles are apparent.

First, you need a force that is stronger than the force holding the injunction or the belief system in place. One way to create such a force is to step up the energy by increasing the vibration of the field. It may be accomplished through shamanistic processes such as the heat of a sweat lodge, the energy of a drumming ritual or the force of a dance. Regardless of how the field is generated, it needs to be stronger than the force that holds the present form in place.

Second, something needs to release. In a sense, something needs to die. It may be the death of an ego, a belief system, or an attachment or habit. Death and rebirth are part of the process of change.

Third, a ritual needs to have a moment when the participant transcends normal consciousness, breaks their accustomed boundaries and goes beyond their known identity. There is that moment, that special moment, when suddenly you are no longer doing the ritual but the ritual is doing you. You are drumming and drumming, and suddenly it seems that it is not you drumming but the drumming is drumming you. You're out of form; you are beyond or outside your normal boundary or mind set. Something outside you is moving you. You have been transported to an altered reality.

Perhaps you are working with a breath ritual. You have been consciously breathing in and breathing out, and suddenly the breath is breathing you. You seem not in control but are having a true experience of being breathed. You have transcended your normal self and conscious awareness.

Once when I was in China, sailing down the Yangtze River, I met an elderly *qi gong* master who told me that there comes a moment in his practice when his movements become spontaneous and take him over. From many years of practice he had learned to control his mind and was able to observe himself in that altered state without coming out of the experience. He was able to remain in that spontaneous transcended place for long periods of time and, for him, this was the desired goal. If one were to consider his *qi gong* as a ritual, this spontaneous movement would be the sign of the transformed self, the sign of a successful ritual.

I understand that the original yoga postures were actually postures that spontaneously emerged in people who were deep in meditation and in states of nirvana or bliss. A posture suddenly arose of its own accord. Over time this sequence was reversed and people did the yoga posture in order to enter into nirvana or bliss.

An important part of a ritual is having an elder, or a wise experienced person, who can set the stage for the ritualistic event,
oversee the mechanics, look after everyone's safety, and hold the
field. In Zero Balancing, once a practitioner starts to do alchemical
work, she or he must take the role of the ritualistic elder. That practitioner creates the setting for the event, determines the intensity of
the field, how deep to go, how long to hold any fulcrum. It is important to realize that it is difficult for the client to self-monitor when
he or she is in an expanded state. In Zero Balancing, the job of a
ritualistic elder is to monitor the process so the client gets what he
or she needs, in a safe, congenial manner. I add "safe" because all
rituals have an inherent element of danger. There is a risk when
fields are highly amplified, when people get near their edge, or
when a person makes any fundamental change.

The ideas and principles of alchemy and ritual are both about
forming special circumstances to encourage change. In Zero Balancing we have looked at these ideas and have devised methods of
touch that can create special circumstances in order to help promote
and accelerate change.

Mental Containers

One needs to understand *containers* in order to work with energy or
create special circumstances. Containers may be created mentally by
using intention or visualization. They may be created physically
through structure and touch.

In Zero Balancing we create a mental container by "framing" a
session. A frame is basically an agreement between practitioner and
client about what we want to accomplish in a session. Frames may
be implied or spoken, simple or complex, specific or general. In
many situations the frame is self-apparent, as when someone comes
specifically for help with a back pain or with a headache. The frame
is implied in their statement.

Early on in general practice I rarely had people frame what
they wanted because it seemed obvious why they were there. However, as I started to work in domains beyond body pain, I realized
that the frame had a power and affected the potential of what could
be achieved. I began to ask questions such as, "What can I do for
you?" or "What else can I do for you?" or, "What would you like to

accomplish?" I would ask very general questions, and let the person tell me what they would like. Some of their requests were physical, some emotional, some were issues of relationship; others were spiritual, psychic, or otherworldly, such as questions they had about past lives. The possibilities were very broad.

In alchemical work the frame is an integral part of the session and is extremely important. The frame establishes boundaries and therefore constitutes a container and a potential empowered space. The request(s) of the client represents the content. The frame, with its contents, remains present in the field throughout the entire ZB session. All fulcrums will affect its content. As a matter of fact, until the frame is released and the container dissolved, every action or spoken word has the potential for affecting the contents.

A number of strategies make working with a frame more successful. We ask simple questions: "What would you like to address today?" or, "Are there any special things you would like to work on?" There are many examples of this in the reported ZB sessions. As questions evoke the client's response we encourage the use of simple and clear language. Clear requests are more easily influenced than complicated, vague, or confused ones.

The same idea applies to any prayer or request we ask of the universe. It is far easier for nature to "find me a partner" than it is "to find me the love of my life who is six feet tall, blond, who has never been married, and likes to cook." Vibrations sent into the universe will somehow, someday, be met or entrained by nature; or so it seems. A request may be met in unexpected ways and it may not be immediately apparent that an event or thought is a response to your request or prayer. Very complicated requests may take a long time to match or may be met in pieces.

We listen deeply to a person's story. The sense of being heard empowers the person, the session, and the therapeutic relationship. The feeling of having been heard actually has a healing value of its own, in addition to providing information.

There may be more than one request in a frame. Two or three or more things can be accomplished in one session. The principle is to keep the language simple and to arrange requests in an order that is comfortable to work with. If there are a number of varied issues, we look for some underlying principle, or one or two possible common denominators. With this sort of logic and agreement with the client you can establish a domino effect: "If this one thing happened then these other four things can automatically happen."

The positive outcome of a session is more likely to happen when we restate requests into statements that we can "get our fingers on" or ones we know we can accomplish. It is very important to recognize our own limits and abilities. For example, if I can't find a complaint with my hands, then Zero Balancing may not be the best way to serve a person. If someone comes in with diabetes, for example, I can't find diabetes in my hands. I can't find hyperthyroidism. I can't find that level of problem. Homeopathy or acupuncture would be of greater value for this type of complaint, in conjunction with standard medical care.

It often takes creative thinking to frame some problems. Suppose someone says, "I want to be happier." How can I get that request in my hands? How can I find that in the body? Experience has taught me one way to approach this. The underlying idea is that if something feels good it tends to make us happier. I know that if my fulcrum is properly engaged it will feel good to the client. If I can create a relationship between a good feeling and being happier, I am confident that I can address the request of being happier. The fulcrum sets the environment for happiness; the long-term outcome, of course, is up to the client.

Once an older man with many complaints came to see me. His feet ached, his back hurt, he had constant headaches. He said, "I don't sleep well at night," "I'm too gassy," "I have indigestion." There was a long list. He said, "I can't remember the last time I was happy." That statement struck me; it stood out, and seemed far more important than any of his physical complaints. It seemed more an essence issue, a spiritual or soul problem. I asked myself whether addressing the deep lack of happiness would affect his myriad complaints, and perhaps begin a domino effect towards health.

In the ZB session I applied the strategy of using repeated touches that would each feel good. I focused each touch on evoking a pleasant sensation and I asked questions to engage his consciousness. I'd say, "How does that feel?" He'd say, "I don't know." I'd use another fulcrum, and ask, "How does that feel?" And he'd say, "I'm not sure." He just didn't have much connection to his body or a sense of what felt good. I kept working, and after five or six fulcrums I asked, "How does this feel?" And he replied, "That feels kind of good." The moment I got "good" out of his mouth and into the field, I grabbed on to it like a sea anchor and held the fulcrum a bit longer and deeper. The next fulcrum went better. When I asked, "How does this feel?" he answered, "Good." Gradually he got to know the experience of a touch that felt good.

Towards the end of the session, I suggested, "Feel how good it feels to feel something good." I kept building on his experience of pleasure and kept taking him down deeper into his psyche. I guided him further and further into feeling good. Near the last fulcrum I suggested, "Let that good feeling flow through your body." I ended the session with a deep half moon fulcrum to integrate, deepen, and anchor the whole session.

When he came into the office for his next appointment, he actually had a small smile on his face and a slight sparkle in his eye. He still had most of his complaints, but he had turned a corner of igniting his inner being and opening up to hope and possibility. The deeper essence issue seemed reversed. The stage was now set for general improvement of health in all areas.

General possibilities

I like to construct frames with simplicity and order, and in ways I feel that can be addressed through touch. A person may have an attitude or conditioning from childhood which they wish to change. I can work directly with the inner child. Or I can go back to a time in their personal history before a trauma, and amplify the security of that earlier time. The unconscious mind has no sense of time and past events. Whatever arises in the session is in the here and now. These characteristics of the unconscious offer many possibilities and ways to approach a problem.

For example, suppose a person had a very difficult birth and as a result had never felt safe or secure. One possible strategy would be to take their consciousness to a time before birth by asking, "Did your mother have a good pregnancy with you? How did you feel during your gestation?" Interestingly most people will respond directly to such a question, indicating they have an impression from that time: "It felt pretty good." In this case you can say: "Let's go to this time of your gestation and put a fulcrum into your energy body." Since the unconscious is in the present moment, we can amplify our client's experience prior to the difficult birth and thus be in a position to influence their subsequent feelings of security and safety.

A frame can be designed with metaphor or with abstract issues. Perhaps a person has money worries. It may be that the time to pay their taxes is coming up and they're worried about not having enough money. If you can get that issue in your hands and/or put a clearer, stronger field through that worry, you will find their anxiety quotient will drop by some degree. It is amazing. They still have to get the money, but they find they are less anxious.

Once I have clarified the frame, it is counter-productive to hold the frame information in consciousness for the whole session. Left-brain focus tends to block the deeper movement of energy. I release it from conscious thought and just let it act out. Of course I can use specific fulcrums to address the client's stated needs, but every fulcrum will affect the frame to a greater or lesser extent.

Sometimes when working, things come up outside the original frame. I may observe a smile on the client's face and ask what is happening. "Oh, I just remembered the most beautiful moment when I was at my third birthday party." As they relate the pleasant thought I amplify the experience by going deeper, longer, or adding another field to my fulcrum.

Physical Containers

There are many examples in everyday life of physical containers that we use to harness energy: a simple shield around a campfire, the cylinder in a car engine, the shell casing of a bullet or the barrel of a rifle itself. In Zero Balancing I use my hands to create a container.

In building a container, the analogy of cooking and using a pressure cooker is helpful. We use a simple pot and lid to cook. But if we want to cook faster we can convert to a pressure cooker, with its stronger container, clamp-on lid, and valve to release excess pressure.

The pressure cooker image sets a background for how to build an alchemical fulcrum. Three things are needed: heightened vibration, a strong container, and an escape valve. In actual practice the process of heightening vibration goes hand in hand with creating the container. In order to build vibration, a container is needed to hold it. In order to build a container, vibration or tension is needed to define the container. The two events happen simultaneously and work off each other. But for the sake of description, we will look at them separately.

Heightened vibration

There are different ways of building a vibrational charge. I can add more fields to a fulcrum, engage a larger area of the client's body, use more pressure, and/or hold the fulcrums longer.

First, I can add additional fields or dimensions to a fulcrum. The principle is that one field of tension can be superimposed on existing fields and thereby increase the overall tension. Each additional field will provide more usable energy, assuming all preexisting tensions are held constant, and that you build on them. For example, I can place a standard half moon vector by pulling on the lower legs and ankles of a client with a curved pull. I can then add dorsiflexion of the ankles on top of the existing half moon, and vibration will amplify. If I still desire further amplification, I can squeeze the heel bone.

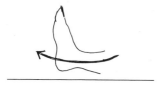

First field created by a basic half moon vector

Second field created by dorsiflexion of the ankle

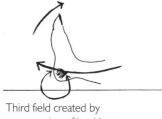

Third field created by compression of heel bone

Compression of heel bone

Building Vibration

A second way of building the charge is to engage larger areas of the client's body. I can use larger surfaces of my fingers or hands in the creation of a fulcrum. Or I can take additional slack from the client's body and the fulcrum will thereby engage a larger area of the person.

A third way of building a charge is simply to use more pressure with my hands or fingers. In this case I am not adding new fields but rather making existing fields more intense.

A fourth way is simply to hold a fulcrum for a longer period of time. Most fulcrums in Zero Balancing are short, one to four seconds. An alchemical fulcrum could be as long as ten to twenty seconds, perhaps even thirty seconds or longer. Because of possible practitioner fatigue and the challenge of holding interface over a prolonged period, extending the time of an alchemical fulcrum requires practice.

Building the Container

Several principles are important in building the container. First, I must stay at interface. Well-defined boundaries are a requirement for building a container, especially as the strength of the vibration increases. As the tension builds, my fingers have a greater tendency to accommodate to the pressures on them and touch sensitivity drops. I need to keep refining and redefining my touch to keep the boundaries at interface.

Second, I work with larger areas of my body and/or engage larger areas of the client's body to strengthen the container. In the example of amplifying the half moon vector, I would strengthen the container by grounding myself more fully both physically and energetically, and aligning myself behind my hands. If I wanted to build a container in the rib cage, I might use the body of my fingers rather than just the tips, or the whole hand instead of just the fingers. Instead of engaging just one or two ribs, I could engage the whole rib cage.

Third, I must stay mentally focused and clear. I need to know exactly what I want to do and pay full attention while carrying out my action. If I think of something I have to do tomorrow, or wonder who my next client is, or even wonder if the fulcrum is going to help, the distraction can weaken the container. The unfocused or wandering mind can take energy away from my hands and away from the container. A quiet, focused mind, with attention and awareness of the sensation under your hands, is an ideal prerequisite for a strong container.

The safety valve

I do not want to overload a person as I build tension in their body. As with a pressure cooker, I want some sort of a safety valve when using these fulcrums. The release valve is a function of my hands and the tension in my body behind my hands. I carefully monitor the client's body signals and if I see signals of overload, I release some tension from my hands or body. I monitor the usual signals of the eyes, the breath, and the voice vitality. I pay particular attention to the face, voice congruity, and the autonomic nervous system.

The subtlest signals to monitor are facial expressions. An expression of either pleasure or concern may be the person's response to the fulcrum or to the content of their experience itself. If I suspect that an expression of concern, worry, or discomfort is from the fulcrum, I slightly lessen my hand or body tension, and see the response.

In conjunction with facial expressions I monitor the voice and the response to inquiry. A person may not be used to the higher charge of an amplified fulcrum, and I want to be sure that the quality of their voice is congruent with my experience of the moment. I have a sense of the fulcrum, in terms of both the strength of the container and the vibration therein. Is the person's response to inquiry congruent with the strength of my fulcrum? Are there any signs of discomfort, indecision, or pleasure? In the first case I would lessen the tension; in the second I would more clearly define the fulcrum; in the third I would prolong the experience.

When people are in expanded states, they will still respond to simple questions regarding whether they are okay with their situation. Their response is reliable, even though the process itself is occurring on a level beneath waking consciousness. They are in unfamiliar territory but they still know whether or not they are okay. If their response is positive, immediate, and with no sign of indecisiveness, I let the process run its course. If I am ever in doubt, I release the process.

Finally, I pay attention to the general signals from the client's autonomic nervous system. I have purposefully and consciously heightened their fields. If I see the heart beating too hard, any unusual breath pattern, or sweat breaking out on the brow (which is the sweat of overload, not depletion), I lessen or release the fulcrum. The color red arising on the face is an indication to lessen tension.

It requires practice to simultaneously contain and build energy as needed for an alchemical fulcrum. The interplay of building and containing the charge is dynamic and each reinforces and amplifies the other. When I feel an appropriate strength of the two, I stop building the fulcrum and hold it stationary for the desired amount of time, carefully monitoring the body signals.

The Bigger Picture

When a ritual is successful there is a spontaneous moment when a person expands beyond his or her usual boundaries. In a ZB session this may happen while the alchemical fulcrum is in place or after its release. Examples of spontaneous experiences include an extended period of expanded consciousness, a release of emotions as laughing or crying, an "aha" realization, a kriya, or a synchronistic event.

Kriya come in many forms. Most commonly in ZB sessions they are a simple jerk-like motion of a muscle, joint, or limb. Occasionally they are more pronounced and lasting, perhaps as involuntary chattering of the teeth. Recently I worked with a gentleman who had a very unusual and fascinating response to an alchemical fulcrum. As I released the fulcrum he began to move both arms in slow random motion, punctuated with non-specific movements of the chest, head, and neck. Amidst this were deep yawns and stretching of the jaws. This process lasted more that twenty minutes. I just observed and held the space, paying very close attention to all signals and periodically asking if he was okay. If I had seen any signs of overload, which I did not, I would have used a simple touch, perhaps on the outside of his leg, to disperse the fulcrum and restore normal consciousness.

Synchronistic events are not uncommon in heightened states and are important in the process. They can come in almost any form. For example, a butterfly flies into the room. The butterfly is a universal symbol of transformation, and if I were working with alchemical fulcrums, I would consider it a signal, sign, or affirmation from nature responding to the content of the moment. It might be a jet plane in the distance, an animal walking by the door, or a leaf simply falling through the air. In the ZB session with Deirdre, we shared the synchronicity of our image of the Dalai Lama, and the church bells rang during the closure of the session. In the session with John, sunlight flooded the room as he was doing deep internal process. Being aware of synchronicities adds a dimension and quality to sessions, and highlights the magic and extraordinary experience of heightened states and of being in touch with all that is.

Integration and Completion

Integration is important after an alchemical experience. Immediately following a session the client needs extra time to integrate the experience. The depth of the session can create momentary disorientation, such as we encounter after waking from a deep sleep. The expanded state of consciousness also promotes vulnerability and perhaps lessened coordination for a short time. I caution the person to go easy, and to walk and drive with extra care.

If the person had a major "aha" experience, or a deep moment of internal processing, a broader discussion of long-term guidelines is often appropriate. A person may have soreness or a delayed emotional reaction when they get home. They may have unexpected tears or anger, or laughter and joy. Sometimes they may fall into deep sleep for a number of hours. These responses are all part of the process of inner shifts, and should be viewed as "healing in action" and allowed to naturally resolve.

Occasionally after such a transformative alchemical experience, there can be a period of sadness. This may seem incongruous because the immediate experience was pleasant or had provoked a long sought-after change. But the sadness may be archetypal in nature. As Lord Byron says in the *Prisoner of Chillon*, "My very chains and I grew friends, so much a long communion tends to make us who we are—even I regained my freedom with a sigh." Something familiar has been lost, and loss evokes sadness.

I advise the client to be extra careful throughout the period of reorientation to avoid accidents, twists, bumps, or strains. On the one hand, there is the temporary awkwardness and lack of coordination that may accompany deep change. On the other hand, if part of the body/mind doesn't quite welcome the change, the unconscious mind may promote an accident to throw the person back into their old natural comfortable configuration.

A person may have a shift of their inner center and have a new sense of self after very deep processing. During the period of fundamental transformations, additional psychological guidance may be appropriate along with further sessions, to support the changes.

Closing

There are many advantages to working with fields of tension that are stronger than our usual day-to-day experience. By intentionally increasing tension we can create what we call an alchemical fulcrum, which speeds the process of change and releases deeply-held imprints from within a person's body. These fulcrums work with the person's own energy and typically the changes that occur are easily integrated into the fields and experience of the receiver. Of course, any time a person makes a fundamental shift within themselves, or a change of their basic value systems, there are some unsteady moments. The outcome, however, is almost always worth the discomfort of reorientation that accompanies change and growth.

Chapter Eleven

Zero Balancing Session with Richard

Fritz: Hello, Richard. How are you doing?

Richard: I think the biggest thing for me is the feeling that change is happening. And, I can't think of anyone I'd rather trust with that change than my magical inner child. My child is still "in touch," has never left "the space," is vulnerable.

Fritz: Is this a special aspect of your inner child?

Richard: It feels to me as if it's the mischievous part of the inner child—the one that just goes ahead, who is there one minute and not the next, but who is always there to herald the unexpected.

Fritz: Hmmmm!

Richard: That, and I need a greater sense of who I am, as a reference point within myself, for the strength I need for this change.

Fritz: You may not know—you don't need to know—but do you have an idea as to what this change may be? Or is this just a feeling that there is to be some change?

Richard: I think it's going to cut across my whole life. *(long pause)* I still haven't found the focus for my life.

Fritz: Steiner says a person doesn't begin their life's work until they are 42. You're just forty two, so rest assured you're right on schedule. *(Richard laughs with Fritz)*

Richard: It's brewing, and the more I witness and see of your work, the more hungry I become for moving single-mindedly into my own depth.

Fritz: Into your own creativity? Your own expression?

Richard: Yes, rather than editing, researching, and publishing a magazine. My feeling is that the change will be something with which I can fully participate and be engaged with. I might be wrong but . . .

Fritz: Let's look at that, open the path towards it, and see where it, and the magical child takes us. Anything else?

Richard: No I think that's the main thing.

Fritz (to everyone): Sometimes, when we're looking for direction and we're not quite sure what we're looking for, one of the strategies can be to let go of anything that obstructs finding your way. Sometimes this can help clear and define the path. We don't always know what we're letting go of but it removes those unconscious things that stop us from seeing the new path.

Fritz walks to Richard's back to begin the opening protocol. As he places his hands on his shoulders, Richard closes his eyes, enjoying the pleasure of it and relaxes into Fritz's hands

Fritz: How many ZB sessions have we done over the last few years? Three?

Richard: Oh at least, maybe more.

Fritz: Do you ever dialogue with the pixie child?

Richard: Yes I do. He comes up spontaneously and giggles. He even tells me jokes sometimes—in the middle of the night—and wakes me up laughing

Fritz motions for Richard to lie down and places a pillow under his head. Richard is still smiling at the idea of consulting the pixie child. As Fritz places the opening half moon in his feet, Richard is very still, very quiet, breathing lightly.

Fritz: All you have to do is enjoy yourself. Let go of all responsibility.

Richard takes a bigger breath as Fritz palpates his abdomen with one hand and holds the lumbar region of his back with the other.

Fritz: It may not be the best analogy but in ancient Greece, several days before a battle, soldiers would receive massage and bodywork. They were carefully tended, so that when they went to fight, they were as fit and supple as possible. I feel at this moment that I am preparing you for a battle; for a battle with change and the unknown. I'm clearing your body to make it really available, supple, and light.

Richard smiles, and nods agreement with the analogy. Fritz makes three passes down the lumbar region of his back, then moves on to the right hip. As Fritz picks up Richard's right leg, there is a deep sigh from him. He already seems far away and deeply in process.

Fritz: I'd like you to have the experience of being tended.

Fritz rubs Richard's knee and places a series of fulcrums there. Then he places a long fulcrum into the gluteal area of the pelvis. Richard sighs deeply and color comes to his face. Fritz then moves to Richard's left hip and repeats a similar sequence.

Fritz (evaluating the left hip): I have the sense of some block in this hip which is in the way of your path. I don't know exactly what it is. *Fritz holds a hip fulcrum.* I'm going to hold an external rotation hip fulcrum and as I do this, I'm going to slide my hand up the inside of your thigh, right here, into the insertion of the gracilis muscle. *(He does so.)* Yeah, right there.

Richard: Yeah, that's it. *(Laughs and releases a huge breath.)*

Fritz comes off the muscle, and rubs Richard's whole leg.

Fritz (checking the hip motion): Yes, that's much better.

Fritz now moves to Richard's left foot and spends a considerable time, feeling, tending, and moving the whole foot area. Then he places a fulcrum in the tarsal area. Richard is in deep apnea, a period where no breathing occurs. He shows working signs in the eyes. He is very quiet and still.

Fritz: How you doing?

Richard: I'm doing good.

Richard's voice is gentle.

Fritz: Tom, would you come here?

Fritz (to Richard): Is it all right if Tom feels this?

Fritz (to Tom): I've been working on this foot a great deal *(indicating the left foot)* and I haven't yet worked on the right. I'd like you to evaluate both feet, comparing one with the other—in particular in terms of the density of the bone and tissue. *Tom feels both feet.*

Tom: This one is very soft *(indicating the left foot).*

Fritz: The left foot was like this before I started *(illustrating how much the left foot has changed in comparison to the right).* Richard has been holding a lot of energy—a lot of tension—in his feet. Upon releasing this, his whole being will feel lighter. Energy will generally more easily move without these blocks. It will have a more spontaneous quality and his inner pixie child will feel delighted. *Richard smiles at the thought.*

Fritz (to Tom): Keep your evaluations in mind as a marker, then come back in a moment and feel his right foot once I've worked on it. *Fritz works on the right foot as he did on the left. Tom returns and feels the right foot.*

Tom: It feels much less dense than it did before.

Fritz places a long, integrating half moon fulcrum into both legs. Richard sighs deeply. He is continually looking more peaceful. His breathing is more regular, more rhythmic, and deeper. Fritz moves to his head and applies a half moon fulcrum to his head and neck. Richard releases another deep breath.

Fritz: I hope your inner child is enjoying the experience.

Richard responds with a beautiful smile. Fritz makes two passes along his upper back, then places a deep fulcrum into the front lower rib cage.

Fritz: I'm going to hold you here. Let your mind assess your inner psyche and if there's anything holding you back from finding your true self, just let it go.

Richard lets out several deep breaths, all of which are increasingly vocalized.

Richard: I think there is a soldier somewhere in me. Somewhere in my knees.

Fritz: I'll go down the knees, release anything I find, and then I'll come back.

Fritz moves to Richard's knees. Richard smiles. There is a loud stomach gurgle. Fritz works each knee independently. Richard's right hand twitches. Fritz then stands in front of Richard's feet. He rests each foot on Richard's thighs, holds the knees from underneath, and works them alternately up and down. A kriya ripples through both Richard's hands. Then he sighs deeply with real pleasure. He seems very far inside himself. Fritz returns to Richard's upper back.

Fritz: Let's continue with the imagery of searching ancestral fields, personal fields, psychic fields for anything that's in your way. There's no rush. You can even search into past lives.

Richard responds to this by releasing a new wave of deep breaths.

Richard: Yes, There's a sense of responsibility. *(Pause)* I think it has something to do with my future. Something I agreed to do a long time ago.

Fritz: Is that an agreement you want to keep, or is that something that's standing in you way?

Richard: No. I think I'm going to keep this one.

Fritz: OK.

Fritz plumps up Richard's chest swiftly and energetically.

Fritz: Does that feel better?

Richard: Yes, thank you.

Fritz: Again, just feel how good it feels to have your psyche clear from things that are in your way.

Richard: It feels very good.

Fritz: Good.

Richard looks as if he is in a delicious state: peaceful, rested, and experiencing great pleasure. Fritz begins to work on Richard's head and neck.

Fritz: You've made some tremendous changes since we first met.

Fritz places a half moon vector through Richard's neck and then slowly draws his right hand over Richard's skull, holding the side of his head with his left hand. Richard appears to be drinking in the sensation. Fritz then holds two points with his thumbs, deep in the leading edge of the trapezius muscle.

Fritz: I suggest that if you have any frustration in the body, because of not finding your path, then let that frustration go.

Richard releases a deep breath, goes very quiet, and lightens in color.

Fritz: And now let the breath energy fill your whole body and sink into your core personality.

Richard's fingertips meet above his chest and form a pyramid, leaving his body a little as if drawing up energy to that area. A kriya moves through his feet. Color shows in Richard's face.

Fritz: Let in any special guides, helpers, Bodhisattvas.

Richard moves his right hand onto his lower abdomen. He again looks serene, peaceful, and very content. He is deep in apnea. Soon his integrating breath seems to complete a particular process.

Fritz: I suggest that you feel and experience a sense of deep rest.

The atmosphere in the room is quiet and still. Richard looks as if he has been asleep for a long time.

Fritz: Let's do a very gentle "nod yes" fulcrum. That's it. And again. And once more. And now relax.

Fritz removes his hands. There is a long pause. Fritz gently stimulates Richard's scalp.

Fritz: I'm getting ready to come out. How are you doing?

Richard: I'm doing very well.

Fritz: Is there anything else I can look at for you, or do for you? Have a look around your body. Are your knees OK?

Richard: My knees feel good. There's something just here. *(indicating his left cheek).* There is also a key point here. *(placing his hands on the front of his rib cage)* I don't know what's happening. See if you find anything there.

Fritz first tends to the left side of Richard's face. Richard lets out a very deep sigh. Then he places both his hands on Richard's sternum and above his heart. A tremendous amount of emotion is released. Richard looks a little sad. Fritz holds the heart area with one hand and places his second hand under Richard's head, creating a head-heart fulcrum. There is a deep vocalized sigh from Richard. He looks as if he is getting what he needs. Fritz plumps-up the shoulder girdle area. A kriya ripples through Richard's body.

Richard: That feels wonderful.

Fritz gives a thumbs up sign to the rest of the group, and remains sitting quietly at the head end of the table and watches, as Richard's breath gradually returns to a clearly-perceptible rhythm.

Fritz: OK?

Richard: Yes.

Richard's voice is quiet. The atmosphere in the room is one of extraordinary silence and peace. Fritz returns to Richard's feet for a closing half moon. Richard is clearly in bliss. There is a long pause.

Fritz (to the others present in the room): I would like each of you to come up, one-by-one, and put your hands on Richard's heart.

Hugh places his hands on Richard's heart.

Richard: Try it all together.

We all go to the table. Six hands are placed over Richard's heart. His right hand begins to shake involuntarily as do his feet. He breathes deeply into the feeling. We remain there a few minutes. Once we move away, Richard gives a sigh of approval. Fritz does several strong, deep fulcrums on Richard's head and neck, and another closing half moon fulcrum on his legs. Very, very slowly Richard begins to move. Carefully he begins to turn on his side. His eyes are closed. He moves with great deliberation, in full control. He eases himself carefully into an upright position. He looks relaxed, rested, peaceful, content. He opens his eyes; they sparkle. He has an impish, cheeky smile on his face. He looks like a Buddha.

Richard: Hi. C'est la vie!

We are all smiling from ear to ear. Richard walks slowly up and down the room and stops.

Richard's report of the ZB experience

I wanted to make full use of the possibilities arising from the session. I decided to concentrate on the strong possibility of change in my life. There are many factors converging in my life that lead me to believe that such change is inevitable. The question was: How to support that change, how to go with the flow?

The ZB session began and I felt my body responding with pleasure to letting-go. When Fritz began working on my feet, it was very evident that the foot still to be "done" was dull, dense, and, by comparison, lacking in life. Fritz called Tom over to compare the radical difference. I felt quite shocked at the difference, especially as I had not noticed any problems or tensions in my feet. When both feet had been worked on and that work had been integrated with a half moon, I felt as if I had a universe in each foot. They felt open and full of possibility, simply radiating life energy. Corny as though it may sound, I also noticed that my third eye was doing a merry little dance in direct response to this work.

When Fritz began to work on my legs, I remember thinking: "Hey, That's not fair Fritz. That's not in the protocol!" But it did feel good. He was working over the top of the leg, working with the tension there and placing fulcrums while twisting the muscles. At this point he said he was reminded of how the ancient Greek warriors were massaged to prepare their bodies before going into battle, only in this case he was preparing me for facing the unknown. It felt good to have a pair of legs for the journey!

Later on, Fritz put in a fulcrum inside my left thigh to the inside of the hip joint. I felt a fire of stored energy there. At first it was slightly painful but soon it began to melt and normalize. It felt like old stuff was dissolving away. It felt good.

As Fritz worked on my upper back, holding me open, he asked me to scan for any non-serving energy hidden anywhere in my body. I looked for any such energy and also for signs that could guide this journey and lead to my future. Suddenly, I became aware of a shadowy, cloaked figure sitting over my right leg. He seemed to be patiently watching the proceedings. I spoke of this to Fritz, and he asked me if this was something to be dissipated. I felt no harm to my body and there was a feeling that I had some past agreement with this presence, almost as if we were old friends or brothers. I felt happy to let him remain there.

As I relaxed into that decision, I became aware of a very sensitive opening above my heart, right between where my hands were resting on my chest. It was so delicate, like a pulsating light. At first I felt very protective of it and began to feel into its fineness, then as I became more attuned to it, it became a golden light that carried such a nurturing warmth to it. I saw it manifest into a golden winged being that descended onto my chest and just held me. I felt so loved. It felt as if this manifestation was linked to a much more powerful source that was being channeled into me, and tears of gratitude began to flow from my eyes. I felt a smile spread across my face in response to these glorious feelings. My smile became the being's smile, and with a playful, mischievous edge to this smile, the being whisked right into my body, turned its whole body around, and began tickling my ribs from the inside! It was a joyful play, and I couldn't help laughing inside.

Fritz then suggested I invite my guides and any Bodhisattvas into the moment. As soon as he said this, more beings swooped in from my upper side. If felt like an inner party was taking place. All were there with great love and my permission. I just allowed the moment, relaxing deeply into my body.

I was aware that various spasms and gyrations were going on in my body. I just let my body do whatever it wanted. I was beyond trying to mentally work-out what was happening. Everything felt good.

Fritz then asked me if members of the group could come and place their hands on me and there was an immediate "yes." As soon as the first hand touched me and withdrew, I knew that more was needed, and I asked them if they could all touch my chest and leave their hands there for a while. I felt that I needed help to contain the dance within my body. Their hands felt like an extension of my own body but I still felt the need for something else, some denser sealing was necessary.

When the group's hands left me, Fritz held my head up and pushed down over my upper chest several times. It felt like the perfect thing to do. The angle was just right and I felt the energy move down my body. Finally, when he gave me a half moon to the feet and held his body against the soles of my feet, I felt properly sealed and even more, I felt proud and happy to be in this body. I felt that this life was a wonderful opportunity.

As I walked up and down by the table, the renewed sense of purpose became more concrete. I felt as if I had received a gift and a blessing. Certainly, I have been left with a greater sense of trust to allow my future to unfold in its own time and its own way.

Chapter Twelve

Experiencing Alchemy

The Opportunity for Change

Alchemy implies magic and the extra-ordinary. In Chapter 10, we looked at ways of building alchemical fulcrums. In this chapter I focus on how consciousness can be shifted through their use and how we can induce non-ordinary experiences. Alchemy is "any magical power or process of transmuting," where transmuting means "changing from one form into another." Alchemical touch can provide extraordinary experiences and even bring one closer to their divine nature.

From a rather simplistic view one could say that, since energy is neither created nor destroyed, we are composed of the vibration present at the beginning of all things. Astrophysicists postulate that creation came from one "Big Bang." If that moment released all the vibration and energy that is Spirit, then our energy is still connected with it and we all have a God or Spirit aspect within us. As Jung has said, "Bidden or unbidden, God is present." As one experiences this reality deeper and deeper one can begin to see Spirit, or God, in everything and everybody.

Spirit is present everywhere. When we come to this under-standing we know that every touch contact can engage that Spirit essence. We can touch a person in such a way as to take him or her beneath levels of fear, anxiety, and uncertainty, and help establish re-connection with their deepest essence. Our intention is not to al-ter a person's inner understanding of spirituality or their belief sys-tems, but rather to facilitate a fundamental experience of optimism, joy, and happiness that resides at that essence level.

At the Esalen Institute a number of years ago Joseph Campbell described three levels of human activity: the first, and best, activity was to experience the Mystery; the second best was to share about that experience; the third best was our actual day-to-day activity in society, involved with science, commerce, formal religions, and the like. Campbell explained that we could not approach the first level using the vocabulary of the third; words cannot capture the Mys-tery. The experience of the Mystery could only be approached through myths, imagery, imagination, or direct experience.

Touch is one of the fastest and often least confusing ways to create direct experience and get beyond the thinking and analytical mind of the third level. Through bodywork we have the opportu-nity to create deep experience and work directly with it. We can open the door to the first level—the personal experience of the Mys-tery, of the Spirit. Herein lie some of the extraordinary dimensions of touch and seemingly magical dimensions of alchemy.

Working from Principles of Nature

Zero Balancing is based on laws and principles of nature, rather than on medical pathology. It is neither diagnostic nor symptom-based nor limited to a desired outcome. The lack of pathology focus gives us the opportunity to work directly with a person's health and poten-tial. Fulcrums become far more than simply techniques to accomplish specific ends or relieve particular symptoms, rather they become in-struments to promote change in accord with one's natural growth process.

This opportunity for change is based on a number of assumptions that have developed out of our hands-on experience. These assumptions progress following the principles already discussed. They are:

- we are connected to and are an extension of nature

- we are an energetic system with a particle aspect that represents our physical manifestation and a wave aspect that represents our inner nature

- the particle nature changes with time and circumstance; the wave nature is continually changing in configuration and yet remains connected with the beginning of all things

- clearer, stronger fields of energy will override or alter weaker fields

- healing is more possible in expanded states of consciousness where people are less held to conditioning, trauma, and self image

- actualization is more possible when fields of the body are clearer, and in better balance and relationship.

Expanded States of Consciousness

With these assumptions as background, I would like to share my understanding of the relationship of touch to expanded states of consciousness. We live in many fields of vibration that are at the surface of life, comprised of our personal conditioning, hectic lifestyles, busy minds, fears and anxieties. We have accommodated to these fields over time so that we are no longer aware of their vibrations. Beneath these surface vibrations we have a more subtle vibratory nature, which is usually obscured from our daily experience. Through touch and expanded states of consciousness we can help a person gain access to this subtle nature.

Rosanna Price, an acupuncturist and Zero Balancer, wrote an essay of her early experience with Zero Balancing"

After years of searching, yearning for a spiritual context in which to place my life, I had my first ZB about 11 years ago. It took me somewhere that I had not visited since extremely early childhood. It took me directly into the presence of the divine. So wonderful was that place, the light, warmth, and unfathomable love and acceptance, that I simply did not want to leave it. I felt that I had been given the key to escaping the drabness and miseries of normal life. That first experience gave me something that has never left me, something which has immeasurably changed my life for the better: the certainty within myself that something higher and better exists, and that nothing can take that knowledge away from me."

Expanded states of consciousness can offer very powerful healing potential. In expanded states, we are less locked into our internal conception of self. We are less identified with our conditioning, problems, or illnesses. In expanded states, beyond linear consciousness, we are more in touch with our holographic nature; we can allow the internal world to shift and expand and more easily reprogram the mind.

I remember so clearly the first time I watched Deepak Chopra on television speaking of the Ayurvedic viewpoint of health and disease. In particular he spoke of the nature of reality, the nature of consciousness, and the nature of meditation. I remember my "Aha!" experience when I realized that with ZB we accomplish through touch what Chopra was describing in words. We can help the client work within their inner world at whatever rate they choose. We can catalyze the meditative experience he described. We are able to facilitate a quiet state of mind for the client in a few moments, one that otherwise might take weeks or months of sitting practice to accomplish.

According to Chopra, meditation allows us to escape "time-bound awareness," to experience unity of consciousness, with no sense of separation or sense of other; and to experience that part of ourselves (the soul or spirit) which is beyond change. He explained that through meditation we could experience the seen and the seer as the same thing, and know ourselves as "non-local." Synchronistic events happen more frequently and anxiety is lessened. We can experience love and the space between thoughts.

Unity and Duality

Chopra's common theme was how to replace experiences of duality with experiences of unity, how to move from the world of two to the world of one. As I listened to him I was reminded of my high school physics class when the instructor gave a lecture about the attraction of opposites. Afterwards he demonstrated how the opposite poles of magnets attract each other while like poles repel. Then a few weeks later he told us that like also attracts like, and gave several examples: a drop of water is attracted to a larger drop and they coalesce into a larger whole. Or on the social level like-minded people are drawn toward one another.

For a long time I wondered how it was possible to live in a universe where opposites attract, while at the same time like attracts like. These seemingly contradictory concepts only began to make sense when I accepted the possibility that we actually live in two different realities at the same time. One reality is unity; the other is duality. One world is not inherently better than the other in that each has its purpose, but each is governed by a different set of rules and provides different experiences.

It can be mind-boggling to grasp that we live in two worlds that occupy the same time and same space, each with different operating principles and experience potentials. But it can be even more mind boggling or confusing not to know this—to attempt to cope with all our experiences as though they were based on the same parameters. Throughout the day we inherently move from one reality to the other depending on the circumstances at hand and the location of our focus. To a greater or lesser extent we have some choice as to which world we are in at any given moment.

Many years ago I was advised to be careful when first opening into unity experience because frames of reference suddenly change, and that if I didn't realize this, things could become very confusing. The most basic values suddenly shift. In the world of duality we are used to judging this and that, and suddenly we don't judge anything. We may be used to thinking this is mine and not yours, but suddenly it is ours or no one's. In the world of duality we selectively love this person or selectively love that person. In the world of unity love becomes a singular experience. We love everything. We love trees, birds, women, men. We are in love with life. It is a very different reality.

I remember an experience during one of my first trips to Esalen. I had come up from the sulfur baths, fully relaxed, open, expanded, without a care in the world. I stopped for coffee in the main dining hall and was just sitting there enjoying the view of the ocean. I had no inkling of unity consciousness in those days and didn't realize that I was in that state. A man came and sat across from me. I had never seen him before but when I looked at him I fell in love. I couldn't believe it. I was stunned. I was overwhelmed by love. I quickly and nervously finished my coffee and left. I have no idea who the person was and never saw him again. But those few moments left me deeply confused. I didn't know what had happened. I had never experienced anything like that. Overwhelming feelings suddenly seemed to come out of nowhere.

I found a satisfying explanation for that afternoon only years later, when I learned more about energy, the kundalini process, and about living in two worlds simultaneously. I was so much at one with everything that when this man came into view, I felt at one with him and therefore in love with him. He could have been anyone or anything and I would have loved it at that moment. I know now that this is, and should be, a wonderful ecstatic place to be. But when it first happened to me I was caught totally off guard and unaware, and without any frame of reference to understand it, I was frightened and confused.

Touch and Unity Consciousness

We can use touch to help a person move from the experience of duality to one of unity or into a meditative state. There are a number of ways to achieve this.

Pleasure and pain

One way of accomplishing movement from duality to unity is by using the polarity of pleasure and pain. I have devised a special fulcrum, the *Hedonic fulcrum*, which employs the sensations of pleasure and pain to induce an expanded state of consciousness. The definition of a hedonic fulcrum is a fulcrum that "hurts good" to the client. In the blue line drawing *hedonic* would be located at the extreme far right end of the box where the sensations of pleasure and pain reside simultaneously.

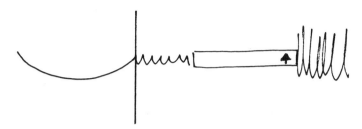

Location of a hedonic fulcrum

"Hurting" and "feeling good" are usually contrasting experiences. In this fulcrum, I hold these polar opposite sensations of pain and pleasure constant in the experience of the client for a brief period. Experience has shown that when the person is confronted with two equal and opposite sensations, they go into an expanded state of consciousness to cope with the experience.

As a matter of technique, it is easiest to create a hedonic fulcrum utilizing bone rather than soft tissue. The ribs are ideal, especially a place on the ribs where an excess of energy exists. This point already is tender to the client. A hedonic fulcrum is created by lifting or pressing deeper into the rib, to the depth that it "hurts good" to the client. Within a few seconds of holding these sensations stationary, the person will go into an altered state.

Filling and Overfilling

Another way we can move from duality to unity is by *filling up until full*. Several years ago a group of us went on a seven day silent trek in the desert of Morocco. The pinnacle experience of the trip was near the last day when we each camped by ourselves in the desert dunes. The design was that we were each to find a location in the dunes, out of sight of the others, where we would camp for 24 hours, utterly alone.

The 24 hours began after we finished our evening meal together. We hiked off to the campsites we had prepared that afternoon. We were to regroup the following evening for our last dinner, when we would celebrate breaking our isolation and our silence.

About mid-morning the following day, I was mediating in my small campsite when a huge wave of happiness just rolled over me. It seemed to come out of nowhere; it engulfed me for a moment and then passed on. I was in bliss, in Nirvana. A few moments later another wave came, engulfed me, and left. After this happened four or five times I asked myself the question, "What would it feel like if my whole body were actually filled with happiness, rather than being washed over by the sensation?"

When the next wave came and began to engulf me, I made a conscious move to absorb the vibration of happiness into my body, as deeply as I possibly could, to the cellular level. It was like filling a glass from the bottom up. I experienced the happiness vibration as it filled me from deep inside and moved all the way up to the more superficial outer me. I absorbed the vibration so deeply into my body that, as it began to fill me up, I became more and more ecstatic. This process took a number of minutes during which I had full awareness on the event. It was wonderful.

Then a very strange thing happened. I was filled with the vibration, like the overflowing horn of plenty, when I began to have an out-of-body experience and lost track of what then happened. The next thing I was aware of was feeling cold, and when I opened my eyes, I was surprised to find the sun had moved far across the sky. Several hours had gone by, of which I had no recollection. As I gradually became more conscious I felt otherworldly, transcendent, clairvoyant, and more transparent than I had ever been. The past, present, and future were one. There were no separations. I sat with those feelings until it was time to break camp and return to the others.

In retrospect, my left-brain interpretation of the event was that I had filled up with one thing totally—in this case the vibration of happiness. I had experientially moved from duality (me and happiness) to unity (me being happiness). The experience of a singular sensation transported me into a meditative state.

Later I pondered the question of how to create this filling sensation for another person through touch. I believe I achieved a partial success by modifying a basic alchemical leg fulcrum. Specifically, I created a larger than usual bolus of energy within the client's leg, and moved it slowly and firmly down the outside of the leg. When I deposited the energy into the fibula, I pressed deeper, held it longer, and got more behind myself with my body mass. All these modifications meant that the stronger vibration went deeper, filling the person's skeleton to such an extent that flushing, heat, and tingling preceded the shift of consciousness.

Merging experience

A third way to create a unity experience is to intentionally merge two separate proprioceptive experiences into a single experience. This is a dependable way of achieving a unity experience because of the characteristics of the nervous system. Information is transmitted through the nervous system utilizing off/on sets of signals, similar to Morse code used in telegraphy. This binary system is extremely efficient for dealing with linear information but not for processing merging experiences. When the linear mode of perception is pressed beyond its capacity, expanded or altered states of awareness can result. If we can develop two separate sensations in the client's body and merge them into one experience, at some point in the process the person will be unable to track the two sensations. As they become indistinguishable the person will move into an altered state of consciousness.

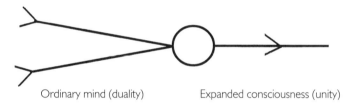

Ordinary mind (duality)   Expanded consciousness (unity)

Introducing a meditative state through merging sensations

    This can demonstrated almost anywhere in the body. For example, I can pick up a client's legs as for a simple half moon vector, and intentionally apply different amounts of tension onto each leg. This creates an asymmetry and two distinct impressions. Beginning with this asymmetry, I slowly add more tension into each leg, while I simultaneously and gradually equalize the leg tensions. By the time a full stretch is developed there is symmetry in the client's body. We hold the tensions for 3-7 seconds and then release. Either during the process, or while holding the tensions, the client will most often demonstrate signs of expanded consciousness.

Meditation Strategies

According to Joseph Campbell in his book *Mythic Image*, there are two ways to meditate: from the perspective of the sixth chakra or the perspective of the seventh chakra. Both methods are effective but they are different. Meditation through the sixth chakra allows recall of the event, whereas meditation through the seventh chakra does not.

From the sixth chakra perspective we focus or concentrate on an external object—a candle, holy image, mantra, breath, or even the tip of the nose. When we focus on an external object, there is an inherent sense of "me" and "other." The separation of "me" and "other" eventually becomes so fine, however, as to be almost non-existent, and a meditative state develops. When the meditation is over we can recall the event because the implicit sense of separation between "me" and "other" persists.

From the seventh chakra perspective, however, we completely merge with the experience and there is no sense of "other." There is only Unity, only the Divine. The "I" does not exist, and therefore there is no one to recall the experience. We know we have gone somewhere, but will be unable to tell you anything of the experience—there is no recollection. Holy women and men from India often report this phenomenon.

Through touch we can approach both these perspectives. I can press into the client's thigh with one finger and hold this pressure stationary so the client experiences my touch. Then by releasing as slight an amount of pressure as possible I reverse the direction of the thrust of my finger. I hold this point for several seconds and then come off. Almost inevitably the person will experience expanded consciousness, because they are unable to track the two conflicting sensations of pressing in and lifting out.

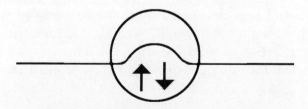

Experiencing equal in-pressure and out-pressure
Inducing "singularity" or "nothingness" through touch

The client's response to our touch determines whether there will be recall of the event or not. The technique centers on working with exactly equal and opposite pressures. In some cases the person will experience this as a singular sensation, in which case there is recall of the experience; in other cases the person will have an experience of zero or "nothingness" with limited or no recall of the experience.

In the above example the therapist needs retain a high level of attention so as not to go into an expanded or altered state his or herself. For some people a variation of this fulcrum may be easier to do. Specifically, I can press into the person's thigh and hold. Then, without changing the tensions, I shift my awareness to the sensation of the client's thigh pressing against my finger. When I experience the exact balance of the *out-pressure* of the client's leg against my finger with the *in-pressure* of my finger into the leg, I have reached a critical juncture and maintain that balance. Even though this is my experience, at the exact moment I have the equality of pressures, the client will go into an expanded state. I can tell this by the body signals. It is easier for me to stay out of an altered state because of the focus I have on the relationship between two things—my fingertip and their thigh.

| In-pressure | Perceiving the out-pressure against the finger | Perceiving the equal in-pressure and out-pressure against the finger |

Inducing "Nothingness" through touch

Working at a Spirit Level

Spirit is a more fundamental part of a person than either mind or body. When we say "go to the spirit level," we imply going to the deepest part of a person. Through touch we can go beneath body sensation or awareness, beneath emotional engagement, and beneath the chatter of the mind. We can engage unity consciousness and engender feelings of transcendent peace and the sense of "being home." Used in these ways, touch has an alchemical potential to produce experiences inherent in the mystical or spiritual life, and thus bring one closer to their spirit and true nature.

Experiencing our true nature

Ramana Maharshi, as well as many other Indian sages, said that a person's true nature is happiness and bliss. They claim that beneath all our conditioning and all our personal mythology, buried somewhere beneath the veneer, lies our true nature or original self.

In ZB we can touch a person at this essence level. Experiences of joy, peace, and happiness indicate that we have indeed engaged the essence level, the true nature of the person. "True nature" exists everywhere in the body and is not limited to one tissue or one place. My preference is to locate it in bone, especially in bones that are easy to feel, like the tarsal bones of the foot or the ribs. I want as little overlying soft tissue as possible so I can feel the bone most clearly.

If I want to look for "true nature" in terms of a rib, I make the best bone connection possible. I reach under the supine person and raise up into the rib cage and explore to find a clear section of a rib. I then put my awareness on the bony aspect of my fingertip and move it slightly back and forth over this portion of the rib, to establish a clear tactile connection. My touch itself does not necessarily go deeper, but rather my awareness of sensation becomes more focused. My awareness of the client's bone becomes clearer and clearer, to a point where I feel that there is nothing other than the essence of bone under my finger. Once I get to that awareness, I feel I am in contact with the essence or true nature of the rib and thereby the true nature of the person. I press deeper to create a fulcrum and hold this for several seconds.

I have treated many people repeatedly in this way and have seen profound shifts of attitudes toward greater happiness and ease. I attribute part of this to the person's recurrent experience of being touched at a core level of their true nature.

Rosanna Price said in her essay:

[...] at present my conscious work with ZB and spirituality has settled down to working normally with people, seeing if anything

comes up for them without prior discussion, and if it does, to nurturing and encouraging the work without doing anything particularly different. I suspect I am only aware of the tip of the iceberg: how much of a person's spiritual life is conscious anyway? Who knows what heights people may be reaching during those blank moments which can so often happen during working states?"

Being in the moment

Touch can help us approach the mystical realm by simply offering an experience of being in the present moment — in the now. In truth all we ever have is the moment, but we rarely *experience* that fact. Our minds are too busy, life seems too demanding, and the past and future too present. Touch has the ability to help us realize Ram Dass' admonition to "Be Here Now." When we literally experience the "now," there is nothing other than that, and we thus find ourselves in unity consciousness.

When a person sits up at the end of a ZB session, he or she rarely looks the same as before the session. The eyes are clear and sparkling, the demeanor is calm, centered, and peaceful, yet alert. Sometimes the person seems dazed or momentarily disoriented. Rarely are they unaffected in some way. The outcome of the session seems greater than the sum of its parts, and I attribute part of this to the experience of altered states of consciousness.

Spirituality into Action

Alchemy, as applied to touch, implies some magic and the extraordinary events resulting from touch. However, the ability to induce expanded and altered states of consciousness does not lessen the magic of the happening. Rather the wonder and awe increase as we see people change from the opportunities and experiences of touch.

When I attended Muktananda events, one by one hundreds of people would go up to him to pay respect and to receive the blessing of his touch by a tap on the head or body with a peacock feather. After paying my own respects, I would position myself in the audience where I could watch people coming away from the experience.

It was astounding. Almost everyone through that line had a reaction. Some were dazed, some were confused, some were in tears, and most had the slightly stunned look of people in ecstasy. Rarely did anyone look the same as they did before being touched by Muktananda. The experience had a discernible effect. From my perspective, the energy body of almost everyone had been somehow affected by that one touch of a peacock feather.

Closing

Touch becomes increasingly alchemical when we can navigate the wisdom and teachings of great teachers from past and present, and translate them into direct experience for someone else. Because ZB is based on coherent principles, we are able to incorporate esoteric concepts in our fulcrums. Throughout the book I have referred to the teachings and philosophies of a number of people—Chopra, Campbell, Young, Grof, Maharshi, Ram Dass, the Dalai Lama, and others—that relate to extraordinary matters. I have tried to show how we can work out their perennial truths and teachings through touch. The fact that touch is so versatile is part of its charm, importance, and magic. Touch gives us a way to approach the Great Mystery. It can put spirituality into action.

Chapter Thirteen

Zero Balancing Session with Deirdre

Fritz: I am looking forward to doing a Zero Balancing with you. Is there anything specific you wish to address?

Deirdre: As a starting place, what I'm really excited by is the totally new body sensation I've experienced since my initiation from the Dalai Lama. I would like to further amplify this sensation, ground it in my bones, and make it even more real and apparent to me.

It's a feeling like joy and like courage, but it has a very oceanic sense to it. It's actually neither about being happy nor being brave. Compared to this feeling, everything else seems like surface currents on the ocean. It is a feeling that everything is absolutely the way it must be. Even though the design of the universe seems so bizarre, so full of suffering and pain, it is nonetheless the perfect design. It's very joyful. I don't want to sound crass but even the perception and understanding of suffering has a joy to it because it's the way; it just must be.

Fritz: It sounds like a deep body-felt sense indicating that everything is really okay.

Deirdre: It's much more than okay. It's absolutely joyful and blissful. It's a feeling of the "Ocean of Bliss." I wasn't expecting it from the practice, I really wasn't, and suddenly there is was.

Fritz: Do you feel this sense other than when you're meditating?

Deirdre: Absolutely. On several occasions, when I expected to be caught by a certain emotion, say grief, there was instead this feeling of joy. It's not that I was denying grief, repressing or suppressing it; it's just that the joy is stronger. I noticed that grief was there but the joy predominated.

Fritz: For this session let us establish some body signal to indicate when you are experiencing this Ocean of Bliss. It is easiest to raise your right index finger whenever you have this feeling. Then, if I see your finger rise, I'll know of your experience and I can either anchor it or amplify it, depending on where we are in the session.

Deirdre: Can we make it either index finger? *(laughter)*

Fritz: Sure, or any signal you care to suggest.

Deirdre: The index finger is fine. I just don't want to get caught on right or left. *(laughs)* I'm not sure why it's important to say this but whenever this feeling of joy is present it is so clear that the only really important thing is the liberation of all beings. It's that kind of joy. The liberation of all beings seems possible, really, really possible.

Fritz: Yes. *Pause.* Anything else? Anything on a personal level?

Deirdre: *Pause.* I'm feeling very well, which is also a great joy. Having felt rather ill since I was a baby, to be able to say "I feel very well" is extraordinary. Umm! However there's something about— how to phrase it?—I no longer care (to use a Fritz Smith phrase) to hide my strength to save other peoples' feelings.

Fritz: Wonderful.

Deirdre: That's the dance that has gone on for me in the last few years. I no longer care to do that because other people's feelings are their feelings.

Fritz: Let me ask you this. Do you ever have the thought: "If only Fritz were here, he could do such and such for me?"

Deirdre: Oh yeah!

Fritz: "Such and such" as . . .

Deirdre: Back pain. Shoulder pain, right shoulder. Head pain at the top of my skull. These last few days my hips have been very sore, which is strange. In the big picture, none of this seems to matter very much, but if I were looking at the small picture, I might think, "If Fritz were here, he'd sort these out."

Fritz: Okay let's go ahead and see where the session takes us.

Deirdre is sitting on the treatment table. Fritz steps behind her and first evaluates the shoulder girdle, and then, going down the back, evaluates the pelvic girdle. He then asks Deirdre to lie down.

Fritz: Remember the finger signal.

Deirdre: Okay.

Fritz picks up Deirdre's feet, and holds them steady for a few moments before doing the opening half moon vector through her legs. When he sets her feet down he walks to the head end of the table, leans over, and says to her:

Fritz: When I picked up your feet, I had a very strong feeling that sentient beings are watching you with an awareness of possible transformation. You have had that vision of transformation and know it's possible. I was sensing sentient beings just watching for that possibility. This doesn't mean that you need to do anything particular at this moment; I'm just sharing my process.

Deirdre smiles, and Fritz goes back to her feet and repeats the half moon fulcrum. He then moves on through the lower back portion of the protocol, addressing the sacroiliac joints, the dorsal hinge and the lumbar spine. He then puts fulcrums to connect the energy of the pelvis with the right hip. Deirdre exhales and relaxes into the inner sensations.

Fritz: Just enjoy yourself. Enjoy being looked after for a few moments — free of responsibility.

He then places fulcrums on the outer side of both her thighs. It looks like it must feel delicious. Suddenly Deirdre's arms fall away from her sides and hang in space — a look of total relaxation on her face.

Fritz (to everyone): I placed a fulcrum into the outer side of each thigh, creating for Deirdre two separate experiences. Holding each of these fulcrums in place, I then calibrated my touch to exactly match both hands, knowing that once my hands felt equal to her, she would have a singular experience and drop into unity consciousness. I then amplified both fields, taking her even deeper into unity. We all saw her physical response to that experience.

He holds the connection and speaks softly to Deirdre: "This takes you to the place of no shadow." He disconnects and comments to the group.

Fritz: If you take your hands away gently when someone drops into these deep states, they will stay there for a few moments. *(pause)* Once you see the hyperpnea breath pattern, you can proceed.

Fritz then puts his hands under her again, integrating her experience by placing more fulcrums onto her sacroiliac joint. Staying with these fulcrums he continues to speak to Deirdre:

Fritz: I want to remind you to recognize how good it feels to be cared for and looked after for a few minutes. How good it feels to really be tended.

He then disconnects from the lower back and, sitting on the table, picks up Deirdre's right leg and places it across his lap. He evaluates the hip motion, and places a standard fulcrum onto her right hip. He then begins to evaluate the buttock area and places a fulcrum onto the acetabular ridge of the pelvis. Deirdre smiles so broadly her nose wrinkles in a beautiful, young crinkle. She has a look of total innocence and joy. Her index finger then raises — indicating to Fritz that she is experiencing that special sought-after body sensation.

Fritz: The synchronicity of the moment was that about two seconds before Deirdre signaled that inner feeling, I looked over to the picture of the Dalai Lama on the mantle piece. As I looked at his photo I was thinking how beautiful he is and how he's enjoying Deirdre being looked after. While I was seeing his image, Deirdre's finger went up — she was experiencing her inner joy.

Deirdre: I'd like to say something. At the exact moment you were looking at his picture, I had the internal image of the Dalai Lama looking at me and enjoying what he saw, just as you said. I don't know whose reality that was but it was absolutely right.

Fritz: We are in the same field.

Fritz touches the outside of Deirdre's leg, and then appears to put a fulcrum just below the inside of the right knee. She lets out a deep breath in response and her fingers raise once more and her arms stretch, open and drop off the table again.

Fritz: Just before Deirdre signaled that she was having that feeling again, I had wanted her to experience the beauty of touch. I had my hand below the knee, so I placed a gentle fulcrum. That's when her signal went up, and she was experiencing that inner feeling.

Deirdre's arms return to her side, and Fritz moves on. He then goes to her right foot and puts a single fulcrum onto the tarsal bones.

Fritz: As I placed this fulcrum I began to experience colors — in particular, purples and greens. *(pause)*

Deirdre retains her relaxed, happy smile. Fritz then sits on the left side of the table and simply lifts her left leg across his lap.

Fritz (to everyone): For the sake of teaching, I want to share with you my inner Zero Balancing process as much as is possible. So many things happen at any given moment that it's impossible to put it all into a linear time frame as they occur. Suffice it to say that whenever I see the finger-raising sign from Deirdre I immediately amplify the field to give her a deeper reality of that moment and help imprint it in the bone.

Fritz then continues to put fulcrums into the left hip and pelvis as kriya shudders go through Deirdre's whole body. He works with his fingers taut and outstretched over the top and sides of her leg. He then finds a place on the inside of her leg, just to the top of her knee. Here he holds a connection and puts in a fulcrum. The smile disappears from Deirdre's face and is replaced by a serious expression.

Fritz: Are you all right?

Deirdre: Yes. Fine thank you.

She breathes through something, clearly encountering something that takes her inner attention. Fritz holds the connection while scrutinizing her face for signs of her inner scenario.

Deirdre: It feels like very troubled water coming up. I'm riding through it, but I'm aware it's fearful.

Fritz: Am I hurting you?

Deirdre: No. It's just that it's quite an interesting dark space that I wasn't expecting.

Fritz: As I started moving my hands through the tissue of your leg, I asked my fingers to contact the water official. For those of you new to Chinese medicine and the five elements, each of the five elements is considered to have an official to oversee the function of the element. The water official relates to fear, anxiety, courage, fluidity, pliability, and fluid balance in the body. I've asked the water official, "What do you need?" The water official says, "I'm very thirsty." I found the place right here *(the spot just to the top of her knee mentioned above)* to release the water essence for the official to drink, and that's when you said you began to feel troubled waters. We are in the same field, so let's just go through it, if that is okay with you.

He presses deeper with the fulcrum. Deirdre exhales deeply.

Deirdre: There's a sense of my heart official helping.

Fritz: Very much. She's holding the boat steady.

Deirdre: Yes. Here's a reference for Tom. *(Tom acknowledges Deirdre.)* The way through troubled water is that lovely story from Thich Nhat Hanh: "You can't frighten me. We'll do it a thousand times if we have to."

Fritz: Mm. Yes.

Fritz continues by going down to Deirdre's left foot, placing another fulcrum. More deep breaths. There are clear bodily signs of Deirdre's inner struggle.

Deirdre: It's strange feeling a lot of fear. But it is just fear. That's all it is, if you know what I mean.

More deep but slow breaths. At one point Deirdre's whole body shudders up through her neck as energy flies through her.

Fritz: Just let it go. We're activating the water principal, the water official, and fear is an integral part of water — you're going to be fine.

Deirdre: It's not a problem. *(she smiles)* In fact it's quite exciting.

They both give a bubbly laugh.

Fritz: It's like the deeply held fears of the water official surfacing. My sense is that it's necessary for the water official to feel more comfortable in her own environment.

Fritz then works both Deirdre's feet at the same time as energy continues to move through her body. He then does a half moon through the legs, integrating all that has gone on and moves to the top of the table.

Fritz sits down and begins to massage both her ears at once. Both Deirdre's fingers raise. Fritz disconnects and a broad smile spreads over Deirdre's face. Fritz then reaches under her upper back. Deirdre licks her lips and her eyeballs roll in their sockets. A look of absolute peace appears on her face.

Fritz: I'm in the mid-thoracic area, and I've put in a fulcrum, which in my perception has taken Deirdre to zero—or should I say into unity. Even though my fulcrum is very deep into her rib cage, she hardly feels me or knows where I am.

Deirdre opens her lips, as if to speak, but the delicious feeling overwhelms her. Her lips soundlessly close again. Fritz looks totally in control and his fingers move a little to a place under the top of her shoulder blades. He holds her steady on both sides. She releases a long exhale. Fritz looks knowingly at the group and says:

Fritz: I'm going to predict that the oceanic feeling of bliss is about to reappear for Deirdre. I'm very deep in the neck on the bone, about the 7th cervical vertebra. Here it comes. *(to Deirdre)* A suggestion? When you feel that feeling, make sure your water official feels it.

A second or two later, Deirdre's head lifts up and back, Fritz disconnects. Deirdre raises her fingers, her hands follow, and her arms are pulled upward and outward into space where they collapse over the edge of the table. Deirdre's face flushes and the inner dance begins again.

Fritz: Time just to wait.

Fritz waits a while, then goes to the very top of Deirdre's shoulders. He pushes deeply with his thumbs, working the soft tissue with his fingers as he goes. He then disconnects. A second or two later, Deirdre's fingers raise once more. A distant chime of bells is heard at that precise moment. They both let out a soft chuckle.

Fritz: That's the water official saying, "Hey I'm getting it."

Fritz goes back to the lower neck.

Fritz: That's much better. There's much less tension.

Fritz then explores the right and left shoulder joints simultaneously. Deirdre's arms go out and her hands open outward towards the back of her arms, holding a certain tension.

Fritz: Too much?

Deirdre: No, that's wonderful. Thank you.

Fritz: Just set down any unnecessary burdens. You have the vision, the possibility, of releasing the suffering of so many beings.

Deirdre: It's absolutely great in the right shoulder.

Fritz then shifts to concentrate on the right shoulder, particularly using his thumbs. He goes in deeply.

Fritz: Just take whatever you need and let go of what you don't.

Deirdre's right arm keeps going back, revolving around Fritz's pressure. She then raises first one leg, then the other, onto the surface of the table. Her hips follow the rotation around the centre of pressure. Her whole body expresses what seems to be a balance of exquisite pain and pleasure.

Fritz: I'm concerned. Am I hurting you, Deirdre?

Deirdre: It's hurting and it's wonderful. The hurt is healing. If you're fine?

Fritz: I'm fine. *(to everyone)* This is a dilemma because I know I am beyond the hedonic point of "hurting good" into a level of sensation that "hurts bad." I know it's a very important area, but I do not want Deirdre to feel abused. It's a delicate dance and I need to know that both of us are okay.

Deirdre It's deep, deep, deep, deep in the bone. It's deep in the shoulder. But what's before my eyes is a very bright, bright sky blue, and I feel good. I feel great.

Fritz: Okay. Work with me. I'll hold this point stationary and you work your body around my hand.

Deirdre: You'll let me know if I'm giving you a problem in any way?

Fritz: I will and you are not.

Deirdre: But you'll let me know?

Fritz: Yes. And you?

Deirdre: It's like a really strong current coming upward from my right hip, up my side, out and down my arm, and through this hand. *Deirdre wiggles the three fingers of her right hand.* There's a lot of stuff pouring out through these three fingers. It's very, very, very strong and I'm not wanting to direct this at anyone, so if anyone is near my hand, please move.

Fritz: No one's in your field.

Deirdre: Good.

Deirdre continues to rotate her whole body. She twists and turns as a reflection of the inner energies pulsating through her. Fritz breathes out repeatedly as he maintains the point. They continue to check that each of them is okay. It looks as if they're both totally locked into wrestling the awesome energies coursing through Deirdre's body. Neither gives up. The center holds and Deirdre continues to follow the currents right to the core. Insight arises.

Deirdre: I don't know what this is but I have the feeling that this is where all my migraines have come from.

Fritz: You okay?

Deirdre: I'm really looking forward to getting rid of it.

Fritz relocates his fingers.

Fritz: Here it is again.

The writhing continues. A point is reached, Fritz disconnects. The journey changes its intensity. She exhales deeply. Her right arm remains outstretched with her awareness now deep within her right shoulder. Fritz lovingly strokes her head. Deirdre's right arm raises again and is then joined by her left arm. She reaches back towards Fritz who connects with the tips of her fingers. A new movement begins as ever so gently the two of them get a hand to hand, finger to finger connection. Fritz stands up off his stool to follow Deirdre's hands right into the air above her body. Fritz supports her hands in his and slowly they disconnect, both beaming broad, loving smiles. Fritz sits back on the stool and there is a long pause. He then asks if there is anything else to do.

Deirdre: There's one small point which still needs attention— right in the middle of my right shoulder joint somewhere.

Fritz: I'll explore a little lower and get my bearings.

He goes into both shoulders and begins to press forward, gradually increasing the pressure.

Deirdre: That's it.

Fritz: Let go into my hands.

Deirdre relaxes and exhales repeatedly, faster and faster. Emotion floods through her. Her face flushes. Her eyes moisten with tears. Is it pain or sorrow? For a moment, her breathing becomes very fast, then she takes a sharp inhalation and lets go. Her head rises chin up and then lolls to the right. Her face holds a pained expression. Fritz closes his eyes and tunes his touch to an even finer degree. Slowly the look of pain is washed away by a look of peace. Fritz disconnects, and Deirdre's head comes into the center once more. Time stops. Fritz strokes Deirdre's head softly and then goes into her upper shoulder once more. Deirdre exhales deeply, a huge release seems to have occurred. Fritz disconnects. Deirdre's eyes open and look up to the ceiling. Her whole body looks totally still and very relaxed.

Fritz: (*after a long pause*) I'm getting ready to close. Survey your body and see if there's anything else you need or want.

Deirdre: I would really appreciate a bit of pressure right here. (*She indicates the top of her head.*)

Fritz works into that area and suddenly a delicious smile appears on Deirdre's face. Fritz moves down to the sacroiliac joint. He puts a fulcrum connecting the sacroiliac and the right hip. Deirdre shows signs of internal movement of energy and her body ripples upward right through then past the neck. Fritz goes down to the final half moon fulcrum through her legs and Deirdre raises her two index fingers to indicate her special place once again. Fritz whispers something softly to Deirdre that is beyond the microphone's senses and she smiles.

He disconnects and stands back. Deirdre smiles deeply and for the last time raises her two index fingers. She slowly sits up and thanks Fritz. Her face is radiant. Gently and with a chuckle she steps onto the ground and walks lightly with a spring in her step. She walks up and down a few times smiling happily and goes over to hug Fritz. In the middle of their embrace church bells nearby begin to sound in harmonious reflection. Everyone laughs uproariously. The energy in the room is palpable.

Suddenly, Deirdre's cat jumps up onto the table, where just minutes before Deirdre had been lying, purrs happily, and starts licking her paws. The energy released is really beyond description. In Zero Balancing sessions it is more than occasionally possible to touch the divine in another human being. When this happens, healing is the natural outcome.

Deirdre's report of the ZB session

Interestingly, I don't have much sense of a continuous narrative for this ZB, though often I do. I was winging it out there in the heavens a lot of the time. But here are a few highlights as they come to mind.

At first, I found it really hard to settle into the session. I was very conscious of other people in the room. But within moments, the lovely image of the Dalai Lama that we have over the mantelpiece, the center point of the room, floated in front of my closed eyes and came into focus about a foot in front of me. At the same time, his voice was saying something very reassuring—though I forget exactly what. So I gave Fritz the pre-arranged signal (the raising of my index fingers) indicating that I had arrived at the feeling—and was very happy to hear that Fritz's experience of the Dalai Lama's image and mine had so exactly synchronized.

Then, there was that strange journey into fear. When Fritz was working on my left leg, it felt lovely, feeling his kind hands on a part of my body that is swollen and always painful. Suddenly, from feeling light and happy, I found myself in very deep, dark waters — not dissimilar to those cold, dark lochs you find high in the Scottish mountains. Rainy, cold, dark, shadowy, and gloomy. It was like surfing beneath the weight of a dark ocean. It was very interesting to feel fear powerfully arising and manifesting in my body, as well as in body movements, yet to feel simultaneously at ease with it.

Then, as it was clearing and the scene got lighter, it was interesting to feel that same energy as excitement. I'm reminded of two things. One is Fritz's explanation that the physiological difference between fear and excitement is whether you are breathing or not — which is a very useful thing to remember and pass along. Secondly, as I'm typing, what's coming up is my childhood horror at that Old Testament story of the Egyptians getting drowned in the Red Sea, when the Old Testament God decided to close it, having previously parted it for the escaping Jews. Now what's coming up is all the confusion of childhood about Judeo-Christian religions and cruelty. I was a keen reader, museum and art gallery visitor, and over and over again I was horrified and confused by the juxtaposition of words about goodness and morality with stories and strong visual images of cruelty and pain.

It was so wonderful to have those severe pains in my upper back and right shoulder given such fine and close and prolonged attention. They've been troubling me for a long while. I can remember that, although the pain was very intense, it was also such a delight to sense the pain that was leaving. And, simultaneously, I was flying through the night skies — whirling and turning. At one point Fritz said something about having taken me to zero — I think — and my own sense was of being a gyroscope spinning in infinity. In fact, two songs were playing in my mind's ear throughout that part of the work. One was the Beatles' *Blackbird* — and specifically this verse: *"Blackbird singing in the dead of night/Take these broken wings and learn to fly./All your life,/You were only waiting for this moment to arise."* The other was a Paul Simon song — the name escapes me at the moment — and the lines, *"Angels in the architecture, spinning in infinity."*

Then, that amazing extra piece on my right shoulder! It seemed such a tiny residual pain that I almost didn't bother to mention it. I'm glad I did. As it unfolded and released through corkscrew-like movements, my mind's eye was flooded with image after image of prisoners and war victims—too many coming too fast to describe. A truly terrible dark sense of world sorrow and of suffering at its most intense and terrifying. We've worked on this theme before—Fritz and his wife, Aminah, and me. They've helped me more than words can say. This felt like the final piece of a long, long, long-carried burden. The instruction to work with the feeling and the vision of knowing (and I do know it) that the liberation of all sentient beings is a workable project, was absolutely spot-on. The fact that it felt correct reinforced for me the sense that my earlier life's work has been completed and a new phase is under way.

I'm very happy the cat came into the room as we came to a conclusion. Happy she came towards me as I did my post-treatment walk. Happy she jumped on the treatment table. Animals know. I was happy too, and deeply honored, to have the presence of dear friends holding the space around us as we worked

Postscript: August 2004

How interesting to read this account of a very beautiful ZB session eight years later, and to have a window on what the incarnation was up to at that time. As I understand it, there's not a cell in my body now that was there then, though some energetic patterns persist, of course. Like water flowing though a river bed where the illusion is that the river seems the same, even though we know that each particle must be different from what was there before.

And what did this specific ZB session offer? This: the body-felt understanding of the essence of the heart sutra. *Form is emptiness; emptiness is form.* What a gift. To be held in the oscillations between form and emptiness that play innumerable times each second, until the distinction between them becomes no longer meaningful. The body-felt experience of a well-placed zero balancing fulcrum, given without the constraints of the egoic mind, is reminiscent of the heart sutra. Free from attachment, aversion, or indifference.

Chapter Fourteen

Internal Alchemy

Someone once asked if you could do Zero Balancing on yourself. Over the years we played with this idea and the possibilities of literally performing self-Zero Balancing. Our success was minimal. But, as we learned to apply the principles rather than the protocol to ourselves, I now say that we can do a very effective though modified self-Zero Balancing. Some of these principles include the relationship of energy and structure, working with the two bodies, using fulcrums, creating clearer strong fields, employing amplified and alchemical fields, and framing past and present physical, mental, emotional, or spiritual issues. The tools and techniques we use include the breath and our internal proprioception.

The view that we have two bodies, one of energy and one of structure, has many advantages. It gives a model through which to understand subtle relationships in the body. With each breath we take there is a dance going on which relates movement to structure, wave to particle. The skeleton responds to each breath. On inhalation all paired bones in the body go into external rotation and all single bones go into extension. On exhalation all paired bones go into internal rotation and the single bones go into flexion. This very subtle response of the skeleton to the breath goes on all the time in spite of any purposeful motions that we make. It is so much a part of us that we are unaware of it. Like gravity, it is so present that we are not aware of its direct experience. But, like gravity, it has important implications.

The relationship of the skeletal movement to the breath activity helps coordinate who we are. If we can heighten our proprioceptive senses and actually become aware of these integrating movements, we have greater ability to mindfully influence ourselves and our lives. I encourage people to develop as much internal awareness as possible.

My own first experience of the subtle skeletal movement came during a period of meditation. I focused my attention on the bones of my face. After my mind and body became very quiet, I experienced the bones just beneath the eye sockets, and felt them swing internally and externally in coordination with the breath. I had intellectually accepted this as a theoretical possibility, but when I first felt it, I found it so strange and disorienting that it brought me out of the meditation. Once I had the experience it was easier to duplicate it. Through this type of exploration we can develop a deeper connection with the background movements of our bodies.

Sit quietly and pay attention to your whole body. Feel your body get larger with inhalation and smaller with exhalation. Exaggerate the breath and the sensations will become more prominent. It feels like a balloon, which expands and contracts a slight amount with each breath. At the core of this bodily sensation are the very subtle skeletal motions of internal rotation, external rotation, extension, and flexion. These coordinated movements help connect and harmonize the greater whole.

Introduction to Breath Energy

The breath is a primary vehicle with which to navigate our internal world. Both the body of structure and the body of energy are related to the breath. On the physical level, the air we breathe stops at the perimeter of the lung tissue, where the blood gases cross the membranes of the lung alveoli to and from the blood. On the energy level, the vibrations contained in the air we breathe also cross the alveoli to and from the blood. From another perspective, however, the energy of the breath is not limited by the physical body and is very much under our mental influence. By means of our thought we can direct the breath energy anywhere inside or outside the body. This is no longer as mysterious as it was twenty years ago when we thought breath ended at the diaphragm. It may seem confusing for those who first encounter the idea of directing their breath energy beyond the lungs, but from the experiential viewpoint there is no problem demonstrating this.

Let your mind relax and pretend that you are breathing into your elbow. Feel what happens. It may take a moment to have an experience. Pay attention to the sensation in the elbow, and continue to breathe in and out of it. There are no right or wrong sensations, but a number of feelings are possible. Sometimes it feels like the elbow is getting slightly larger on inhalation, and then slightly smaller on exhalation. It may feel warm and/or tingling. It may feel like the elbow is somehow more a part of you or it may even seem highlighted in your consciousness. It may even seem like the elbow is moving in response to your breath.

Let the breath imagery go and then compare the feelings of the two elbows. The attended elbow may seem lighter, stronger, fuller, warmer, or clearer than the other. Irrespective of any exact description, if you felt any difference between the two elbows you have been successful in directing breath energy and are beginning to gain more conscious control over your body.

When you first experiment with internal process, it is helpful to work with other people or in a small group. Since energy and its effects are something that we cannot readily see or tangibly touch, there is the perennial question as to whether experiences are "real" or a "figment of the imagination." When we share our experiences with other people, it makes our own more real and tangible. It also gives us the opportunity to hear other people talk about their experiences. If they have felt something similar to us, we feel validated. If their experience is different, it gives us another option for other possibilities.

There are a number of exercises that can be done to increase this type of breath control. As you breathe in and out of the elbow, feel the energy moving down your arm. Or breathe in and out of any painful area in the body, and experience the lessening of pain. Or you can simply stretch the body with the breath and feel it expand further when breathing into the area under stretch.

Parallel Breath Meditation

The parallel breath meditation is a simple yet powerful and versatile meditation. Its purpose is to organize and create harmony within the fields of the body. This is accomplished by breathing breath energy between the crown of the head and the base of the body. It is called the "parallel breath" because the lines of energy passing through the body are parallel to one another, even though (in a sitting position) the breath energy is moving vertically between crown and base. It is the parallel nature of the moving field that establishes the order and harmony in the body and produces feelings of calm and organization.

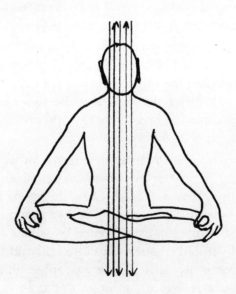

Parallel breath meditation

Basic technique

Seat yourself comfortably, breathing normally. As you begin the meditation you may either inhale the first breath down through the crown of the head and out the base of your body and then exhale up from the base and out through the crown, or inhale the first breath through the base of your body up to the crown and then exhale from crown down to base. Either is fine. They are equally effective. Experiment with both options and see which you prefer. Let the breath energy move through your physical body as it will, without mentally directing it along specific meridian pathways or through specific physical structures.

After several breaths, put your attention onto how the breath energy feels as it moves up and down through your body. If your mind drifts, simply go back to feeling the breath as it moves though you.

Continue for as long as you wish but certainly for more than several minutes. It is not uncommon to devote an entire 15–30 minute meditation session to the parallel breath. As you end the breath meditation release the sensation of the breath energy, breathe several normal breaths and then bring your attention to your base. Feel stable in your base and grounded before opening your eyes. Simply feeling the breath on inhalation and exhalation will organize your internal fields and have a calming, clarifying, grounding effect.

Working with the breath energy—internally

If you wish, you can actually "work" with the breath energy during the meditation. Once you feel the breath energy moving through your body, and that feeling is well established, place an issue somewhere within your lower abdomen or pelvis. As you continue to breathe the breath energy through your body, it will either flow around or through the issue. Continue to breathe, feeling and observing the breath motion.

You know the meditation is working when a change occurs. The issue may become less dense, change shape or color, or even disappear. Any alteration is an indication that the meditation is being successful. Once change has begun it is a judgment call as to how long you continue to breathe the breath energy through the event. A good guideline is to continue the process until the change has become stable. You do not have to wait for the whole form to dissipate—this may be asking too much from one sitting meditation. A significant change that becomes stable is the feedback you are waiting for.

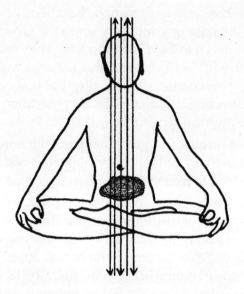

Working with the parallel breath — internally

To close the meditation, let the imagery of the event go, and breathe three or four or more breaths through your body to clear the field. Then put your attention on your normal breathing for several breaths, and finally let all breath imagery go. Bring your attention to your base, feel stable and grounded, and then open your eyes.

Working with the breath energy—externally

You can work with an event or issue that is not yours—perhaps the illness of a friend or some world event. If you wish you can work with these outside of your physical body but within your own auric field. Specifically, once you have opened the meditation and established the feeling of the breath energy moving through your body, move the feeling of the breath energy out in front of yourself. Create a vertical breath movement in your auric field, as though there were a column in front of your body, but not touching your body. Clearly establish the feeling of the breath moving in an organized pattern and then place the issue or event in front of you low down in your auric field.

Work with the event as described above, just letting the breath itself flow around or through the issue, until you get the feedback signal that change is occurring. Stay with the process until you are ready to stop. Then release the imagery, breathe several clear breaths until you are sure that the area in front of you is cleared, and then bring your breath energy awareness back into your physical body. Bring breath energies through yourself until you are clear on the physical level. Then close the meditation as described above by breathing several normal breaths and then becoming stable in your base and opening your eyes.

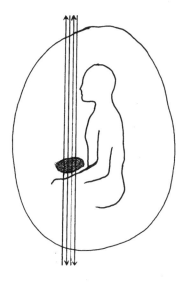

Working with the parallel breath — externally

Technique comments

The imagery of a tide pool is helpful in understanding the effects of this meditation. On a very calm, still day there may be no currents moving, and the seaweed and other plant life seems to be floating in the water with no apparent sense of order. They appear to move randomly.

Then, as the currents begin to move, we see the seaweed sway to and fro, responding to the currents as they move in and out. The movement of the seaweed develops an organized appearance, with even the leaves of the plants moving parallel to each other as they responded to the currents. The movement of the tide puts a sense of order into the tide pool.

So it is within your body. As the breath energy moves through your fields, they begin to become less random or hectic, more organized, with a parallel, harmonic quality. You may begin to experience your body as more clear and open, and your mind become quiet.

You can work with any of your own personal events or issues within your physical body. You can effectively work with other people's issues or world events either inside your physical body, or outside your body, but within your auric field.

Be sure to stay at interface while doing this. This applies to physical, emotional, mental, and spiritual boundaries. At the end of the meditation, clear all fields with pure breath energy before leaving them. And be sure you are stable and grounded in your base before opening your eyes and ending the meditation.

Use the parallel breath to work with problems of the world. It has a special power. I believe that working with world problems in this manner actually helps the world situation. But equally important, it provides the personal experience of doing something for the world situation and helps dispel personal feelings of impotency, victimization, and fear.

The first proof of effectiveness of the parallel breath meditation will be the immediate changes you feel, the calmness of mind and body. Further proof comes over time as you witness improvements of personal issues you have worked on. Once these proofs are real for you, experientially known as fact, you can then take it on faith that the larger fields, such as the world's fields, are also being affected and changed by your efforts. You may find yourself even less fearful, more potent, and generally happier in knowing that your efforts have helped make a change in the world.

Inner Smile Meditation

The parallel breath meditation works primarily with fields, generated by the energy of the breath. Another way of doing internal work on yourself is to create a mental fulcrum and then to specifically move it throughout your body. I didn't understand how to create internal mental fulcrums until I learned the Taoist meditation of the Inner Smile. This was introduced to me through the work of Mantak Chia and provided the basis to work internally with fulcrums. Later in this chapter I will give guidance for doing this meditation.

The smile has a similar form to the half moon vector of Zero Balancing. The smile gives us the natural structure of this fulcrum, with the additional variation that it moves in two directions at the same time.

Half moon vector   Inner smile fulcrum

Inner smile fulcrum

The energy to drive the fulcrum comes from the breath. We have already seen the inherent movement of the body when we breathe. If we consciously couple the breath with the smile, every time we inhale or exhale the smile fulcrum changes shape. When we inhale the smile deepens; when we exhale the smile becomes more shallow. The fulcrum becomes active on inhalation and rests with exhalation.

The relationship of the inner smile fulcrum and the breath

We now have a fulcrum form and the energy to drive it. The only task left is to place the fulcrum. We have already developed the idea that we can direct the breath energy anywhere in the body. There is no reason why we can't direct this fulcrum to wherever we wish. Assume you want to work with your liver. Focus the breath and the smile into your liver. As you breathe in, feel the liver stretch. As you breathe out, feel the liver relax. With your focused attention you have created movement within the organ. You have created an active fulcrum in the liver.

There are several keys to success. When you place a fulcrum, attempt to *feel* its presence within the organ or structure. Make this an exercise in proprioception rather than visualization. What I mean by this is that you should actually *feel* the movement of the fulcrum in the organ and not just visualize it. It is through proprioceptive awareness that these fulcrums are the most effective.

Another key to success is to make a meaningful number of fulcrums in any one place before moving on. There is no exact rule as to the number. If it is a routine fulcrum, with no specific agenda, three to five breath patterns may be enough. However, with problematic areas, fifteen or twenty may seem appropriate. As you work with the fulcrums, you will find you own pattern of working. Follow that.

All this is of huge importance because it means you can consciously affect your own organs. You literally get inside and improve the physical function of the organ. Bringing a moving field into the liver, for example, will improve the flow of blood, lymph, and all fluids; it will release congestion and bring more vitality and vibration into the organ. It helps to have as much anatomic knowledge of any part as possible. Read books on anatomy and look at pictures and diagrams. Get a deep association with the part. I suggest that you look at pictures of normal anatomy, rather than of pathology. You want to work with images depicting health.

I had a problem of tinnitus — a ringing sound in my ears. I reviewed the anatomy of the ear: the outer ear, eardrum, middle ear and the three small bones (the incus, stapes, and malleus), inner ear, cochlea, and eustachian tube from the back of the throat to the middle ear. Once I knew the detailed anatomy, I began to work with the smile fulcrum. I often spent half an hour on the ears themselves. I would smile into the tympanic membrane, the incus, stapes, and malleus. Then I would do a smile into the function of the three bones working together. I smiled into the cochlea, taking the smile all the way up to its tip. I breathed a smile into the eustachian tube. Then I would bring a smile into the function of the whole ear and into the ringing itself. My tinnitus improved over 80 percent.

There are so many variations and possibilities of working with these fulcrums. For instance one can tip the angle of the fulcrum. It can work side-to-side, front to back, top to bottom. It can even be rotated into a twisting spiral type form, if that configuration seems needed. In working with the eyeball for example, you can position the fulcrum to work in the plane of the eye from side-to-side, and then position it in the plane from front to back, then top to bottom. It is even possible to work on diagonal planes. If there is known eye pathology, such as glaucoma or cataract, I could only recommend doing these exercises with the approval a physician.

For instance if I had glaucoma I can imagine having my pressure checked and then, unless advised against it, doing exercises every day to see if I could bring the pressure down. This is verifiable. Or if I had a cataract I can imagine having an eye doctor establish a base line and then experiment with putting a fulcrum into the cataract itself to promote micro motion, and into the fluids of the eye to promote a healing environment. I would do the exercises several times a day and be reevaluated in several months. Again, changes are verifiable.

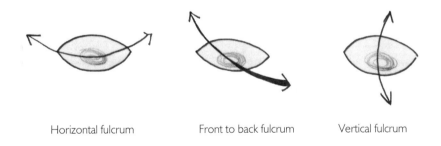

Horizontal fulcrum   Front to back fulcrum   Vertical fulcrum

Possible eye fulcrums using the Inner Smile

Pay attention to both how well you feel and to how the physician's objective measurements read. The subjective and objective worlds can change independent of each other. You could feel better and have no objective change; or you could have objective improvement and not perceive any improvement yourself.

Beyond structure

There are also dimensions beyond the physical organ or structure that we can alter. We have talked of tissue-held memory. Working with fulcrums in the organ can release recent or old entrapped memories and vibrations. This is also true of recent and old held emotions. Chinese medicine tells us that specific emotions are held in specific organs. For instance, in the liver the emotion is anger. The influence of the fulcrums in the liver will help release anger and frustration, whether it is recent or old, conscious or unconscious. It will even release blocked creativity, a frequent precursor to frustration and anger. Using fulcrums in this way is like cleaning house of recent and old debris.

It is important to keep in mind that these fulcrums are powerful, and can result in an emotional release or upheaval. Be prepared to stay with the emotions that come up and to keep in touch with their source during this process. Be mindful of where the turmoil is coming from. If what comes up is particularly intense you may need a friend to talk to during the process. If you do not understand that healing reactions can come up you might be caught off guard. Even therapists who are familiar with this process, or who have already done a lot of work on themselves, can be taken by surprise due to the potency of the inner work.

Another application of these fulcrums is in reference to surgeries. Assume a person has had a gallbladder removed and has long since been discharged from care. Let us assume that this was a needed procedure, that it was very well done, and that the person has felt immeasurably better ever since surgery. This is not an uncommon scenario. However, the best of surgeries leave scar tissue. Breathing fulcrums into the new or old surgery site will increase the circulation of blood and other body fluids in the area, which will promote better local tissue health. Miniscule movements will also be generated in the area, which will have a limbering effect on the scar tissue.

Even though the surgery has removed the physical structure of the gallbladder, since we have two bodies, the etheric or energetic gallbladder still remains. If we looked into this person's initial gallbladder problem we might find a strong genetic tendency for gallbladder pathology and/or a history of excessive fatty food indulgence.

These factors could certainly represent the cause of the problem. But it is also possible, actually probable, that there were additional factors in the energy body such as suppressed and buried emotions and memories that helped promote the dysfunction. These forces remain even after the physical organ has been removed. In other words, part of the cause of the problem still exists.

When you breathe a fulcrum into a surgical site, pretend that the organ is still present. This will influence the surgical site as well as the old buried vibrations in the etheric organ. Many of these will release and the person will have more completely healed themselves from the entire organ dysfunction scenario.

It is possible to heal even more deeply. Most people have little emotional attachment to the gallbladder. But it is an entirely different situation if a woman has had a hysterectomy or a breast removed, or if a man has lost a testicle or had an amputation. Breathing fulcrums into the structure as though it were still present allows us to release emotions arising from the initial cause as well as those that came from the aftermath of the procedure itself. And finally, and perhaps most important of all, breathing fulcrums into the etheric organ gives us the opportunity to reclaim the organ in our psyche and have the feeling of being whole again.

Beyond working with specific organs and the etheric body, working with internal fulcrums is also effective to help with functional syndromes such as chronic constipation, irritable bowel, premenstrual tension, insomnia, and so on. There are no specific procedural outlines for these syndromes. Simply follow the basic principles, be creative, and work out a strategy.

Develop a good working relationship with the fulcrum. Have a sense of the number of breath patterns that are good for you under varying conditions, and know how to move the fulcrum around the body. Be able to perceive the fulcrum movement within the organ site. When you deal with a syndrome, learn as much as you can about the related anatomic structure, the physiology of the parts involved, and perhaps even your own personal history of the problem. Then put this all together in a meaningful way.

If constipation were the issue, one might breathe into the ileocecal valve, the ascending colon, the transverse colon, the descending colon, the sigmoid colon, and into the rectum, anus, and anal muscles. Breathe into the frustrations of being constipated. Breathe into the joy of not being constipated. Reference as much relevant anatomy as possible and create as many relevant associations as possible. Breathe into each of these areas as long as it feels right for you, feeling the fulcrum movement as you do. Repeat this daily and see what happens. Be your own judge as to its effectiveness.

It is very beneficial to work with well-functioning organs as well. Here the Taoist Meditation of the Inner Smile is brilliant. In this scenario the meditation leads one through the whole body, following the five-element model of Chinese medicine. Mantak Chia has worked out a most effective meditation. He mentions this in several of his books. I refer you to *Taoist Cosmic Healing by* Mantak Chia (Healing Arts Press, 2003). I have been using the Zero Balancing interpretation of the Inner Smile for more than ten years and it is one of the most effective meditations I have done. For the first several years I performed it five days a week. Now I may do it once a month.

There are many advantages to following the five-element model in this meditation. It organizes the sequence so that it follows the natural movement of energy within nature and within the body. This model allows one to include the emotions, color, sound, and even movement. I have included a brief outline of the meditation to indicate its flow and scope. However if you are interested in pursuing this I suggest you refer to Mantak Chia's books for a more in-depth guide.

The last thing to say before I outline this meditation is that there is a short form and a long form. The short form may take about 20 minutes. You go through the whole cycle one time. In the long form you go through the whole cycle three times in one sitting. By the third round, you are so clear and open that you will come across things on the repetitions that you didn't realize on the first round. It takes you deep, deep, deep into your psyche. The long form may take you an hour or hour and a half. I suggest the short form five days a week and the long form, say, once a month. After several months of the practice you will find your natural rhythm with the process.

Inner Smile Meditation: the Practice

You can do the Inner Smile Meditation either sitting or lying — so be comfortable!

Inner Smile Meditation

"Begin with the color white.
Into your brow, bring a white color and a smile.
Into your sinuses, bring a white color and a smile.
Into your lungs, bring a white color and a smile.
Into your large intestine, bring a white color and a smile.
Into your skin, bring a white color and a smile.

"Moving on to the color blue.
Into your brow, bring a blue color and a smile.
Into both your ears, bring a blue color and a smile.
Into your kidneys, bring a blue color and a smile.
Into your bladder, bring a blue color and a smile.
For men, into your prostate gland, bring a blue color and a smile.
Into your bones, bring a blue color and a smile.

"Moving on to the color green.
Into your brow, bring a green color and a smile.
Into your eyes, bring a green color and a smile.
Into your liver, bring a green color and a smile.
Into your gallbladder, bring a green color and a smile.
Into your nervous system, into the brain, and into the nerves of the body,
    bring a green color and a smile.
Into the ligaments and tendons of the body, bring a green color and a smile.

"Moving on to the color red.
Into your brow bring, a red color and a smile.
Into the tip of your tongue, bring a red color and a smile, signifying telling the
    truth, knowing the truth, being the truth, living the truth.
Into your heart, bring a red color and a smile.
Into the coronary arteries that supply the heart, bring a red color and a smile.
Into all the arteries and veins of your body, bring a red color and a smile.
Into each and every red blood cell in your body, bring a red color and a smile.
Into your small intestines, bring in a red color and a smile.

"Moving on to the color yellow.
Into your brow, bring a yellow color and a smile.

Into the base of your tongue, bring a yellow color and a smile, signifying the savoring of life, the tasting of life, the enjoyment of life.

Into your spleen, bring a yellow color and a smile.

Into your pancreas, bring a yellow color and a smile.

Into your stomach, bring a yellow color and a smile.

Into your breasts, bring a yellow color and a smile.

Into the lymphatic system and the lymph nodes, bring a yellow color and a smile.

Into each and every white blood cell, bring a yellow color and a smile.

Into your muscles, bring a yellow color and a smile.

"Moving on to the color purple.

Into your brow, bring a purple color and a smile.

Into your pituitary gland, bring a purple color and a smile.

Into your pineal gland, bring a purple color and a smile.

Into your thyroid and parathyroid gland in your throat, bring a purple color and a smile.

Into your thymus gland, located beneath the sternum, bring a purple color and a smile.

Into the Isles of Langerhans, those cells in the pancreas gland that make insulin, bring a purple color and a smile.

Into your gonads, the ovaries, and testes, bring a purple color and a smile.

For women, into the fallopian tubes, uterus, cervix, and vagina, bring a purple color and a smile.

Into your adrenal glands, sitting on top of the kidneys, bring a purple color and a smile.

"Moving on to the color saffron, the color of the monks' robes in Thailand, that beautiful saffron color.

Into the brow, bring a saffron color and a smile.

Into your adult personality, bring a saffron color and a smile.

Into any worries, physical problems, or difficulties, bring a saffron color and a smile.

Into your inner child, bring a saffron color and a smile.

Into your core personality, into that part of you beneath the conditioning and the veneer, bring a saffron color and a smile.

"In closing the meditation, move on to a silent Om.

Into your brow, bring a silent Om and a smile.

Into your body, mind, emotions, and spirit, bring a silent Om and a smile, to coordinate all of the parts we've looked at into one well-functioning, magnificent, beautiful whole.

Letting all imagery go, sit with yourself for a moment and just be.

Then, in your own timing, open your eyes and come back to the here and now with a smile."

Pyramid Meditation

The final meditation I want to mention utilizes the form of a pyramid. This meditation was introduced to me by Aminah Raheem. The procedure itself is straightforward and is designed to create a container in the form of a pyramid, in which you can work with issues, wishes, or intentions. It can be used by the individual to create an empowered space for meditation or problem solving. It can be used by couples or families to work with issues. It can be used for meetings or workshops to enhance effectiveness, as well as organize and frame events.

The pyramid creates an empowered space. It becomes increasingly real and powerful when you engage your proprioceptive channel and give the experience a tactile reality. Pay close attention and you can actually feel a palpable change in the environment when the pyramid is first formed. A level of quiet, increased density occurs that was not there before.

Technique

From a sitting position, drop a line of energy into the earth and ground yourself from the base. Then bring your attention to your coccyx. Draw a line of energy up through your spine to the top of the head, to the crown chakra. Connect with your higher self. Then take your attention up to an apex point in the sky, and from there create a pyramid.

Pyramid meditation

What you place within the pyramid or how you care to work with it depends on the situation of its use. If it is for a meeting or workshop you can empower the space by putting in intentions such as encouraging insights, new ideas, or individual creativity. Whenever we use this in a group we have the injunction of holding one another in the highest personal regard.

When you are ready to close the meditation, bring your attention to the apex of the pyramid and, from there, draw a line of energy down to the top of your head and through each of your chakras in turn. From your base, feel connected between heaven and earth, and at the same time centered and grounded within yourself. Finally, bring your attention solely to your base and let all imagery go. Sit for a moment. Then open your eyes and come back to the present moment. The pyramid is now in place.

In a meeting or workshop setting leave the pyramid and all its injunctions in place throughout the program. If it lasts longer than one day, each morning reinforce the pyramid over your time together. At the close of a program we dismantle it by having a round of applause dedicated to its release. The vibration caused by the clapping disperses the vibrations that have been held in the form of the pyramid. This frees the space.

Closing

The meditations of the parallel breath, inner smile, and pyramid have proved to us that we have the ability to help program and affect our own future. The world is malleable. Our thoughts, actions, and fulcrums seem to influence the unfolding of events. With this view of the world, and with knowledge and experience of how to navigate in the unseen fields, it is possible to make moments alchemical and help co-create and influence the present and the future. This gives all of us greater potential and greater responsibility regarding our own lives, and those of our friends, community, and the world as a whole. We can individually add to the collective in ways that will improve our future and that of all people on the planet, as well as the planet itself.

I want to end with the well-known Vispassna *Loving Kindness Meditation*.

Create a pyramid and make this an alchemical intention for each of us and for all mankind.

Loving Kindness Meditation

May I be happy and have peace of mind

May I be healthy and strong

May I be free of suffering, and safe from internal and external harm

May my life be of ease and well-being

May I have a compassionate heart filled with loving kindness

May I be free

May all beings be happy and have peace of mind

May all beings be healthy and strong

May all beings be free of suffering, and safe from internal and external harm

May all beings have a life of ease and well-being

May all beings have a compassionate heart filled with loving kindness

May all beings be free

Glossary

<u>Acetabular ridge</u> – the dense portion of bone on the upper surface of the hip socket (acetabulum).

<u>Acupoint</u> – a vortex of energy, which is an entry point into a meridian pathway.

<u>Aka</u> – palpable, tangible psychic energy.

<u>Alchemical Fulcrum</u> – a fulcrum of heightened vibration or tension.

<u>Anterior Superior Iliac Spine</u> – the most forward protuberance of either wing of the pelvic bone. It is the insertion point of the inguinal ligament.

<u>Ayurvedic</u> – an Indian (Asia) system of holistic healing.

<u>Blending</u> – reference to fields of energy, it is overlapping of boundaries or areas of energy.

<u>Chakra</u> – literally means "wheel" or "circle." A center of psychic energy, of which there are seven major centers associated with the human form.

<u>Collagen</u> – an albuminoid, the main supportive protein of skin, tendon, bone, cartilage, and connective tissue. Collagen has piezoelectric properties.

<u>Dantien</u> (Tantien) – major centers of energy in Chinese energy physiology, of which there are three: the Lower, Middle and Upper Dantien.

<u>Darshan</u> – the Indian (Asia) tradition of paying respect to a guru or teacher.

<u>Dorsal hinge</u> – the twelfth thoracic vertebra. This vertebra has the unique design of the superior facets being in an oblique plane and the inferior facets being in the vertical plane.

Dorsiflexion – backward flexion or bending, as of the foot or hand.

Dowse – to search for something (underground water, metal, or some unknown thing) using feedback signals from an external or internal agent (divining rod, finger signal, or other source).

End range of motion – a term in joint physiology indicating that portion of joint motion in which the ligaments supporting the joint have been engaged by the movement of the joint.

Extension – a movement that brings members of a limb into or toward a straight condition.

Flexion – the act of bending or the condition of being bent.

Foundation Joints – a classification of joints in the body, which have more to do with transmission of forces than with movement or locomotion. They are characterized by having a small range of motion and no direct voluntary control. The major foundation joints are the cranial sutures, the sacroiliac joint, the tarsal joints of the feet and the carpal joints of the hand.

Fulcrum – in Zero Balancing, a specific field of tension used to implement change that is created with the hands and/or fingers.

Ida – one of the three major nadis, which runs on the left of the sushumna. It is the white, "lunar" nadi.

Ileocecal valve – the valve at the junction of the end of the small intestine (ileum) and the beginning of the large intestine (cecum).

Interface – in reference to fields of energy, it is the juxtaposition of energy fields with clarity of boundaries.

Intertarsal – the articulating surfaces between the tarsal bones.

Kriya – an involuntary body response or movement caused by the resistance to the passage of energy through dense or congested areas of the body.

Kundalini – the serpentine latent (sleeping) energy, located in the Muladhara (first) chakra; the cosmic (female) energy that manifests along the spine and within the chakras.

Meridian – an qi energy pathway in acupuncture and Chinese medicine.

Nadi – a channel of subtle energy. It is said there are seventy-two thousand nadis or energy tube-like canals in the body.

Non-local – at the subquantum level, in quantum physics, all points in space become equal to all other points in space. A specific location is irrelevant.

Osteoblast – a cell that is associated with the formation of bone.

Palpation – the act of examining (the body) through the touch of the hands or fingers.

Periosteum – specialized connective tissue covering bone.

Piezoelectric – electricity engendered by pressure.

Pingala – one of the three major nadis, which runs on the right of the sushumna. It is the red, "solar" nadi.

Pranayama – spontaneous involuntary breaths incited by the movement of energy within the body. Pranayama may also denote voluntary breathing exercises.

Protocol – in reference to Zero Balancing, the format of a Zero Balancing session.

Rolfing – a hands-on-the-body system of therapy named after its founder, Ida Rolf. The system focuses on the relationship of the body to gravity, and on the fascial tissues involved in that relationship.

Sacroiliac joints – the articulations between the sacrum and the iliac (pelvic) bones.

Samadhi – a superconscious rapturous state of meditation.

Semi-foundation Joint – a classification of joints in the body, which have characteristics of foundation joints, but which are less pronounced. They have to do with transmission of forces as well as movement. They have small ranges of motion with some voluntary control. The major semi-foundation joints are the intervertebral joints, the costovertebral joints, and the costosternal articulations.

Shaktipat – transference of psychic energy from master, guru, teacher, or universe to disciple or person.

Signature – identifying characteristic(s).

Streaming – transference of energy from one person to another.

Sushumna – the supreme and most important of the three major nadis; the central channel, which runs through the center of the spine.

Tarsal Bones – the seven bones that comprise the tarsus (the region of articulation between the foot and the leg): the calcaneus, talus, cuboid, navicular, and the first, second, and third cuneiforms.

Tensegrity – an architectural and energy concept developed by Buckminster Fuller. A tensegrity system is characterized by the relationship of continuous tensional forces with discontinuous compressive forces. It is the basis Fuller's geodesic dome.

Tension – a relationship between opposing forces.

Unwinding – the process of unprompted physical movement. A term used in the Upledger somato-emotional release system of therapy.

Upledger Institute – a teaching and clinical facility in Florida, organized around alternative health care systems of therapy and, in particular, craniosacral therapy as developed by John Upledger, DO.

Wolff's law – a change of function in bone is attended by alteration of its internal structure.

Working – in Zero Balancing, the process when energy and structure in the body are interacting to establish a new relationship or balance.

Zero Balancing – a mind body system of therapy designed to balance body energy with body structure, formulated by Fritz Frederick Smith, MD, in 1973.

Zero Balancing: an overview of a session

> Zero Balancing is done through clothing. An average session takes 30 – 45 minutes. Zero Balancing follows a specific protocol. The session begins with a seated evaluation of the client's shoulder and pelvic girdles. The client then lies down on his or her back for the duration of the session. The protocol continues with a curve tractional pull on the legs, evaluation and

balancing of the lower half of the spine (specifically the sacroiliac joint, dorsal hinge and lumbar spine), both hips, and both feet. A curved tractional pull is reapplied through the legs to integrate the changes that have taken place.

The practitioner then moves to the head end of the table and evaluates the thoracic and cervical spine, shoulders, and scapulae. The following period is devoted to balancing the upper back and neck. The session concludes with the balancing of the arms, and integrating the changes of the upper and lower back. A final curved tractional pull on the legs integrates of the whole session. The person remains on the table for a few moments to experience the integration and changes, sits up carefully, and finally walks to regain all bearings.

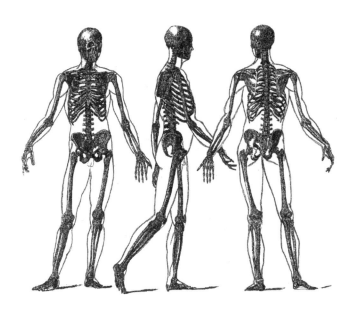

Index

spiritual maturity, 93
split-level consciousness, 9
stimulation of bone to affect spirit, 50, 51
structural body, 36
structural integration, 7
structure and energy bodies, 2, 42, 43, 71, 65
structure and vibration, 45
structure body, 173
  engagement of, 43
subliminal clearing, 70
subtle vibratory nature, 149
Subud, 19
Subuh, Mohammad, 19
sushumna, 108, 196
Swami Muktananda, 11-13, 15-17, 19, 160
synchronicity, 19, 164
synchronistic events, 134, 150

T
Taoist meditation, 181
tensegrity, 37
tension, from over-responsibility, 116
tension, in the bones of the pelvis, 57
third eye, 17
thought, as a wave form, 47
tinnitus, 182
tissue imprint of thoughts and emotions, 48
tissue–held memory, 9, 45, 70, 184
touch and healing, 19
touch as influence on spirit and vitality, 50
touch to activate a meditative experience, 3
touch, as a portal to the Mystery, 148, 149
touch, depth of, 76
Transcendental Meditation, 11
transpersonal psychology, 18
trauma, 93, 129, 149

trauma or accident involving bone, 93
traumatic imprint, 45

U
unconscious mind, 129
unity consciousness, 151,-154, 158, 164
Upledger somato-emotional release system, 196
Upledger, John, 46, 196

V
vibhuti, 19
vibration and structure, interrelation and interaction in the human body, 16
vibration and the subtle body, 18
vibration held in the vertebrae, 105
vibration, excess held in the bone, 70
vibrational fields and behavior, 50
vibrations held in the background field, 95
vibrations stored in soft tissue, 94
vibratory deficiency in bone, 77
vibratory excess, 77
Vispassna, 190

W
wave and particle nature of energy and structure, 44
wave aspect and spiritual manifestation, 149
wave aspect of the body, 42
wei qi, as a vibration, 39, 40
working state, 118
world healing, 3
worldview as imprint, 90
Worsley, Professor J.R., 9, 10

Y
yoga, 52
yoga postures, 125
Young, Shinzen, 3

About the Author

Fritz Frederick Smith, MD, is the founder of Zero Balancing, a body/mind system of healing designed to integrate body energy with body structure.

Licensed as an MD, DO, and Acupuncturist, Dr. Smith practiced general medicine for 15 years before changing his focus for the next 20 years to Chinese acupuncture and Zero Balancing. He retired from active practice in 1991 to devote himself to further developing and teaching Zero Balancing.

Dr. Smith teaches internationally, has written numerous articles, and has authored two books: *Inner Bridges, a Guide to Energy Movement and Body Structure,* and *Alchemy of Touch, Moving Towards Mastery Through the Lens of Zero Balancing.* He lives with his wife in Borrego Springs, California.